STAYING WELL WITH
GUIDED IMAGERY

BELLERUTH NAPARSTEK

WARNER BOOKS

A Time Warner Company

Warner Books Edition
Copyright © 1994 by Belleruth Naparstek
All rights reserved.

Warner Books, Inc., 1271 Avenue of the Americas, New York, NY 10020

Visit our Web site at http://warnerbooks.com

Ⓦ A Time Warner Company

Printed in the United States of America

First Trade Printing: December 1995

10 9

Library of Congress Cataloging-in-Publication Data

Naparstek, Belleruth.
        Staying well with guided imagery / Belleruth Naparstek.
            p. cm.
        Includes bibliographical references and index.
        ISBN 0-446-67134-7
            1. Medicine, Psychosomatic. 2. Visualization—Therapeutic use. 3. Imagery (Psychology)—
Theraputic use. I. Title
RC49.N37
1994
615.8′51—dc20   93-41846
                                                                          CIP

Book design by L. McRee
Cover design by Diane Luger
Cover illustration by Robert Crawford

A CRITICAL DIAGNOSIS: IT'S RAVES FOR
STAYING WELL WITH
GUIDED
IMAGERY

"ONE OF THE MOST EXCITING, PRACTICAL BOOKS AVAILABLE for learning to utilize the remarkable power of your mind to optimize your physical and emotional health. Everything you need to know about creative imagination, from medical research to Belleruth Naparstek's excellent scripts, are provided in this clear, compassionate, and comprehensive resource."

—Joan Borysenko, author of *Minding the Body, Mending the Mind* and *Guilt Is the Teacher, Love Is the Lesson*

"USER-FRIENDLY . . . pulls together everything that currently is known . . . and shows the reader how to use it for good health and growth."

—*Milwaukee Journal*

"ACCESSIBLE AND COMPELLING. . . . Offers many interesting insights into the realm of the subconscious."

—*West Coast Review of Books*

"MORE LIKE AN EXCITING JOURNEY THAN A BOOK. Your guide, Belleruth Naparstek, is surefooted, experienced, and very creative. Throughout the book she can introduce you to rich, unknown inner worlds of imagery that are both rewarding and health-promoting."

—David S. Sobel, M.D., coauthor of *Healthy Pleasures* and *The Healing Brain*

"A WONDERFUL AND LUCID ACCOUNT of the theory and practice of guided imagery . . . a hopeful book that not only understands the relations of mind, body, and spirit, but shows practical ways to use the whole self to find health. Both practitioners and the general public would do well to read (and use) this book."

—Mark Warren, M.D., M.P.H., assistant professor, Department of Psychiatry, Case Western Reserve University School of Medicine, and author of *The Making of a Modern Psychiatrist*

"*VERY* WELL DONE: CLEAR AND CONCISE. . . . In a warm, intelligent voice, the information and exercises are presented simply and understandably. They are eminently do-able!"

—Anne Simpkinson, editor in chief, *Common Boundary* magazine

For Art,
my husband, pal, paramour, and hero—
with boundless love and gratitude.

ACKNOWLEDGMENTS

I hope this book helps a lot of people. If it does, it's because it's been shaped from the ideas, vision, hard work, and big hearts of many others. I'll try to name some of them.

First, I thank my teachers, who helped me understand the substance of what imagery and healing are about: Rosalyn Bruyere, Stephen Levine, Pat Rodegast, Kenneth Pelletier, Barbara Brennan, Emilie Conrad-Da'oud, Deepak Chopra, Robert Becker, Itzhak Bentov, Candace Pert, Eugene Gendlin, Stanislav Grof, Barbara Brown, Milton Erickson, Elmer and Alyce Green, Patricia Norris, Brugh Joy, Roberta Delong Miller, Chogyam Trungpa, Jeanne Achterberg, John Welwood, Thich Nhat Han, Carl and Stephanie Simonton, Tom Cutolo, Bryan Christopher, George Melton, and Wil Garcia.

Next I thank all the physicians, psychologists, nurses,

ACKNOWLEDGMENTS

my fellow social workers, and all the other health professionals who took the time and trouble to give me feedback and check my work for accuracy. Some took the risky position of publicly supporting my efforts in spite of anticipated skepticism from colleagues, and I am especially grateful to them for their courage and kindness. Thank you to Stephen Zinn, Gail Larson, Ronald Strauss, Gail Bromley, Paul Van Ness, Eileen Durham, Julie Lusk, Tom Cutolo, Lucille Eller, Stefan Ripich, Dorothy Siminovitch, David Sobel, Jacquie Rogers, Arthur Newman, Cathy Conheim, Donna Brooks, John Carey, Vivian Bochenek, Henry Bloom, Ann Williams, Charles and Anne Simpkinson, Nancy Wadsworth, Mark Warren, Sallie Lybarger, Roy Szubski, Ann Scott, Sue Thom, Alan Bachers, Michael Lederman, Dorothy Sawyer, Larry Dossey, Howard Hall, Jim Block, Lynne Norrie, Cathy Witt, Susan Zatick, Debra Vail, Barbara Trauger-Querry, and Nancy Elizabeth Nimmich.

I'd also like to thank all the imagery experimenters from among my clients, students, consultees, workshop participants, and tape listeners who educated me further with their feedback via letters, calls, and even conversations in the supermarket line. I'm especially grateful to Joanne Zuroff, Judy Hart, Elaine Szemplak, Jane Oeschle, Sue Ross, Silvia Kenneweg, Bea Lucarelli, Patricia Spaeth, Hannah Pokempner, Melissa Jones, Beth Pritchard, Laura Savelli, Mary Staley, and Andrea Hahn. And I remember with a smile Sandy Cohen, Kathy Light, Wil Garcia, Judy Glassroth, John Paustian, Tim LeBar, Joan Rosenberg, Larry Kolke, Jo Selden, Stan Marks, Archie Drost, Susan Jaffe, Rob Thomas, and P. J. Fisher.

I thank the charming, brainy (both erudite *and* savvy), and very special Tom Grady for first encouraging me and getting me started. Tom also found me Loretta Barrett, my ingenious and generous-spirited agent, who helped me shape this book with her exquisitely honed instincts and her unwavering honesty, intelligence, and enthusiasm; I thank Larry Kirshbaum, president of Warner Books, for his infectious elan, and his vision and gutsiness in buying this book sight unseen because he heard my audiotapes and trusted his intuition; I thank Joann Davis, my smart, responsive, reliable, and thoroughly professional editor, and the whole supercompetent, hardworking, warm-hearted, good-humored crew at Warner, including the sales reps, who especially buoyed me with their enthusiasm, understanding, and energy.

I thank the people at Image Paths who produce my audiotapes and support my work: Barry Rothschild, for his dedication and commitment, his guts in taking such a crazy job in the first place, and his ability to shape it into something viable; Mike Sutila, who understood right away what I was trying to do, and first made it happen; all the wonderful people at Klein News, the parent company that spawned Image Paths, and especially Sam Boswell, Marge O'Malley, Georgia Dorsey, Marilyn Judd, Chris Andreano, Linda Rothschild, Scott Chase, Dawn Farr, Carrie Stewart, Ron Clark, Dan Horowitz, Carol Matelski, Queenetta Burgess, and Angela Zivkovitch, for always being so willing to take the time to help. And most of all, George Klein, who made it all happen with his good instincts, deep pockets, sound advice, evenhanded judgment, brilliant acumen, and impeccable sense of timing and fairness.

I thank all the talented people who helped us create the tapes and build the business that produces them: Bruce Gigax, Bob Lewis, Janis McCormick, Stan Koenig, Susan Small, Scott Cowen, Caren Goldman, Jim Sollisch, Harlan Miller, Melissa Harris, Joyce Rothschild, and of course, our incomparable composer and musician, Steve Kohn.

ACKNOWLEDGMENTS

I thank my dear friends, whose emotional support cushioned, protected, and buoyed me, helping me over the usual anxieties and aggravations: Bob and Joanne Lewis, the amazing Rena Blumberg, Judith Cohen, Vera Lawrence, Elaine Stevens and the whole gang at Roth Stanley, Cynthia Gale, and of course, the stalwarts who patiently listened to the bulk of my whining (not counting my husband, who, without question, gets first prize): Sarah Pokempner, Janet Crate, Roberta Tonti, Dorothy Siminovitch, and Tom Cutolo.

I thank my wonderful family, my sister Carol and her husband Mike, my brother Michael and his wife Sandy, and my sister-in-law Annette and her husband Allan, who warmed and touched me with their steady support, kind encouragement, and inspiring example.

I thank my parents, Olla and Harry Krepon, now long gone but with me all the time. The left brain explanatory segments of this book come to you courtesy of my mother; the right brain imagery exercises, my father. I salute Olla for her grit, and Harry for his kindness. They were people to emulate.

I thank my sensitive, smart, decent, funny, wonderful kids—Aaron, Keila, and Abram, who light up my life, keep me honest, make me laugh a lot, and always remind me of what really matters.

And last and best, I thank my husband Art, steady as a rock, always in my corner, encouraging, goading, inspiring, coaching, applauding, supporting and ingeniously, miraculously, and gloriously making all things possible.

Cleveland, Ohio
November 6, 1993

CONTENTS

CONTENTS

INTRODUCTION AND OVERVIEW

I've been a psychotherapist for over twenty-five years, and I still love what I do. Psychotherapy is work that relies heavily on a trustworthy, powerful relationship for its context, and I find this requirement eminently satisfying. To this day, I'm delighted and a little surprised each time someone honors me with his or her secrets. And when I see my clients begin to gather in their strength and start to move toward their dreams, my heart soars. I know how lucky I am to love my work this much.

Some of my clients are people who have been traumatized, haunted by terrible events from their past. I see people who have been beaten, abandoned, and raped, people who have survived accidents and catastrophes, and people who have simply withstood too many losses in too short a time. The emotional range of their responses to such trauma tends to cluster at one of two extremes: either

1

they are in intense, near-constant anguish, requiring tremendous energy just to negotiate their way through a normal, waking day; or else they are numbed-out, anesthetized and isolated, fogbound and disconnected from themselves and others. Psychotherapy gives them a place to share the horror with someone who won't shrink from it (no pun intended) and enables them to look with some compassion and a measure of detachment at their own suffering. This in and of itself can be a great relief. But too often there are limits to what the "talking cure" can offer people in the face of such enormous suffering.

I also work with people who suffer in more subtle ways, what some of my colleagues have called the worried well. People come to my office who are tired of being driven by self-defeating behavior patterns that get them into trouble time and time again. These are the people who find themselves in frequent abusive relationships. They are the ones who, in spite of great loneliness, persist in fleeing from intimacy. They are those who can't assert themselves and those who manage to offend nearly everyone. I see people who can't tolerate needing anyone and those whose individuality disappears into a relationship the minute it turns sexual or romantic. My clients are the people who can't stop worrying and the ones who don't worry when common sense says they should. When they come to see me, they know they are ready to change something about themselves and their lives, even if they don't know exactly what it is or how to do it. The structure and discipline of psychotherapy provide the support, tools, and feedback to help them do so. Some people change incrementally, slowly and steadily. Others take off like a rocket. Some don't change at all. And most advance in fits and starts, the plateaus being just as important as the times of obvious growth, even if they don't feel that way at the time. But the work is hard and painstaking, and sometimes very discouraging. For some, traditional psychotherapy takes much longer and costs far more than what they initially anticipated.

And finally, quite a few of the people I see are physically sick with debilitating or life-threatening diseases. They come to my office very frightened and undone. They are people with lupus, heart disease, or M.S., looking for help in coping with the emotional impact of their diagnoses. They are people with cancer and HIV infection, eager to try new ways to extend the length and quality of their lives, hoping to reduce their symptoms and combat their illness. They are people who have suffered from a stroke or heart attack, looking for technical help in their struggle to slowly and painfully work their way back to some measure of functional normalcy. They are people who are terrified of an upcoming surgery or chemotherapy procedure, who want psychological tools to help them marshal their courage and optimism to meet the dreaded appointment day on their calendar. All of them are looking to get out of the uncomfortably passive position they find themselves in. They don't feel good about themselves simply taking their medicine, following medical advice, and hoping for the best. They want something more proactive and concrete to do for themselves. They are looking for a new skill to master, something they can take home and try when they wake up with a start at 3 A.M. feeling terrified and alone. For this group especially, standard psychotherapy often isn't enough.

Over the last several years, I've come to rely heavily on a technique called guided imagery, because it seems to be so helpful to all three categories of people I have just mentioned. It can help surface the terrible images of trauma from the past and then provide the balm of new images that soothe and heal; it can speed up the process of psycho-therapy by eliciting spontaneous new insights and fresh, creative solutions; and it can empower the physically sick with a whole new bag of useful, potent tricks that can be pulled out whenever they are needed.

Guided imagery is a kind of directed daydreaming, a way of using the imagination very specifically to help mind and body heal, stay strong, and even perform as needed. This might mean conjuring up images of a tumor shrink-ing or of blood pressure slowing down; it might be images of the emotions growing calm and steady in a safe, pro-tected setting; or it could involve "rehearsal" images of a successful performance outcome, such as, in the case of a stroke survivor, having a right side that moves more the way you want it to do.

As might be apparent from some of these examples, by "images" I don't mean strictly visual images, but any sensory impressions: sights, sounds, smells, taste, or touch. For some, sound may be the most evocative sense they possess; for others, it might be touch or sight.

Of course, therapists work with images all the time. We all were taught, or else we learned on the job, that when we work with our clients' images, and not just their thoughts and ideas, we get information that is more accu-rate and pure: rawer, truer; less edited and reconstructed by the arbitrary selectivity of memory and cognition.

I remember one woman I worked with, Donna, a phobic thirty-year-old—smart, mouthy, and the proud possessor of a riotous sense of humor—who had multiple difficulties in love and work and could no longer bring herself to drive on the highway. Her phobia was making her life difficult and was limiting her options. She couldn't remember much about her childhood, though she often made joking references to her "crazy" family, alluding to a "funny uncle" and an aunt who was mean as a snake. After several weeks of talking, important images began to spontaneously pop into her awareness. At first they would come as a simple fragment: Initially, it was a flash memory of the feel of the side of her face on a cool, white-tiled bathroom floor (later determined to be in her aunt's house), and seeing the base of the tub and toilet from the floor. When this image came up for her, her whole body immediately tensed, and her legs began to shake violently as she became flooded with terror. Her eyes darted about, and she kept standing up and then sitting down again, saying she didn't know if she could stay in the room. It was clear from her intense physical reaction, not to mention the unique sensory detail of the image, that she was reexperiencing what she had felt as a helpless, terrified, violated child.

That image and the ones that followed led the way to helping her heal from the deep wounds of her childhood, wounds that had been so buried under all her words and jokes and reinvented family history that they'd been virtually unreachable before. And what helped her stay in the room, and allowed her to tolerate reexperiencing such horror, as more and more sadistic sexual abuse got uncovered, was not just the strength of our relationship, which, of course, was essential, but the technique of guided imagery as well.

We had agreed that when our work got to be too much for her to bear, she would tell me, and we would stop. I would then guide her back in her imagination to her favorite childhood place, her grandmother's farm in the summer, her sanctuary, where it had always been safe and loving. As she recalled it in all its full, rich sensory detail, summoning up all the sights and sounds and smells of that farm, she would become calm again. Over time, she got very skillful at exercising this option, jokingly referring to her ability to switch from terror to peacefulness as "channel surfing." Knowing she could do this gave her the courage and stamina she needed to continue looking at her life and making the changes that were necessary. Eventually, she even managed to drive her four-wheel onto I-90, all alone save for the company of her very large, rambunctious dog.

This is not an unusual case story. Every therapist has many from where that one came from, because imagery is as much a part of our daily currency as thoughts, words, and feelings are. In my practice, as I and my clients became more and more intrigued and impressed by the power of imagery, I gradually moved into working with it more directly and proactively. As clients were able to identify their own healing images, I began making individualized audiocassette tapes for them to take home and listen to once or twice a day. The repetitive listening to the tapes seemed to intensify and speed up the work of therapy. And it offered comfort, solace, and hope.

At the same time that I was becoming more intrigued by the power of images and their healing potential, my practice was changing. More and more, local physicians and therapists were sending me people with life-threatening illnesses, who wanted help either managing or transcending their physical condition. One such client was Bonnie, who had an advanced case of metastasized breast cancer that had spread into her bones and lungs. She'd been told by a well-meaning but misinformed friend of hers that maybe she'd gotten sick because she'd been too passive, an erroneous idea that was in vogue at the time. Actually, Bonnie was one of the most assertive people I'd ever met. In fact, it would be fair to say she was downright *outrageous*, but got away with it because she was also warm, generous, and kind, with an unwavering loyalty to her friends. In any case, here was Bonnie, determined to beat her cancer by doubling her efforts at aggressively demanding what she needed.

One of the things she decided to demand was a personalized guided imagery audiotape from me, filled with images of her cancer being vanquished in an idiosyncratic, Bonnie-esque way. And she wanted it finished in time for her to use for her upcoming chemotherapy treatments at the Ireland Cancer Center of University Hospitals of Cleveland. When I suggested she might find a good relaxation tape at a bookstore, she made it clear that it had to be *me* narrating these images on the tape, because she was used to my voice and liked it.

Not one to argue with a woman who, if her oncologist was to be believed, had only six months to live, I made Bonnie her tape. I hoped it would give her a feeling of being more in control and less fearful, and help make her chemotherapy treatments go easier on her. And I was certainly aware that the imagery, along with the chemotherapy, might help fight the rampaging progress of her cancer. I took comfort from the fact that at least it would do her no harm. Her oncologist assured me that, if nothing else, it might help her general frame of mind, reminding me that no one at the hospital was exactly taking bets on Bonnie's longevity anyway.

The tape turned out to be about fifteen minutes long and had an assortment of images on it, all generated by Bonnie, then scripted by me, edited by her, then recorded by me. We had her white blood cells surrounding her lesions and shrinking them; there were images of Bonnie being snuggled in her beloved father's lap, feeling all safe and cozy; we had her at her favorite beach, where gentle waves of blue-green healing cleansed her inside and out, taking the cancer out with the tide; and we had her mom, also no slouch in the aggression department, and when she was alive, a ferocious cleaner of things, wielding a vacuum cleaner, sucking up any cancer cells unfortunate enough to cross her path.

My inexperience and my third-rate tape recorder notwithstanding, the tape was a hit. Bonnie carried her portable cassette player with her everywhere, listening to it constantly and religiously plugging it in at each and every chemotherapy appointment, despite the bemused if tolerant stares from onlookers. She listened to it in the waiting room and in her treatment cubicle, smiling beatifically all the while. In very little time, she was telling patients, staff, and anyone else who would listen that they, too, should be listening to guided imagery audiotapes.

Bonnie did awfully well for an astonishingly long time. Her attitude was upbeat, and she seemed to be enjoying life more than ever before. Although she, like everyone else I've ever known, became very upset when her hair fell out, she otherwise sailed through chemotherapy with little or no discomfort. And some of her tumors were shrinking, while others were being held at bay, to a degree that was far beyond her oncologist's expectations. She also seemed to be pain-free, which was strange, given what was going on in her bones.*

As a result, Debra Vail, a gifted and committed clinical nurse on the chemotherapy unit at Ireland, asked me to produce a more general tape to help others on the floor. She was particularly interested in something for people sitting in the highly charged space of the waiting room,

---

*Bonnie stayed this way, strong, energized, productive, and enjoying life, for two and a half years, five times longer than predicted. Her downturn coincided with some traumatic family news. She died after slipping into a coma from a rapidly growing tumor in her brain.

where the extended wait for lab results, to determine whether someone could tolerate another dose of chemicals, often left patients and their families anxious and upset. Given the experience with Bonnie, who was feeling so empowered and optimistic, so free of side effects, and so relentlessly upbeat, Debbie wondered if perhaps a tape wouldn't do the same for others. By then, many of the nurses and social workers were intrigued. Indeed, so was I. Because even if Bonnie was a very special case, she was surely showing us all something about what was *possible*.

So I made a tape for the unit, this time interviewing doctors and nurses, along with patients and their families, trying to get a sense of the universal images that would work for most people. I wound up creating imagery of a beautiful, beneficent fountain of sparkling, healing liquid, hoping this might make the whole process feel more friendly. In addition, the magical fluid from the fountain had a powerful effect on the cancer itself, mobilizing white blood cells and shrinking and desiccating tumors. Other images were included to generate a sense of energy returning and symptoms subsiding. To combat feelings of isolation and fear, I surrounded the listener with an imaginary, magical cheering squad of committed allies. And for good measure, I included what I now know is called end-state imagery, imagery of how a person ultimately wants to look and feel. I found some background music that I thought was evocative and peaceful and made ten copies for the unit.

In most cases, we found that my amateurish tape was helpful. Debra and her colleagues didn't keep research-quality records, but their clinical assessment from their day-to-day eyeballing of their patients was that anywhere from one-half to three-quarters of the patients who tried listening to an imagery tape got some measure of help from it. And of those, somewhere between a half and a third became hard-core enthusiasts. It seemed that when people liked it, they *really* liked it, and credited it as having tremendous positive impact.

Most dramatic was the observable reduction of anxiety, both before and during treatments. The nursing staff also felt that a decent number of people seemed to be physically less reactive to treatment, reporting less dizziness, nausea, depression, and tiredness. This was not altogether surprising. Research as early as 1982 at Vanderbilt University by Jeanne Lyles, Thomas Burish, Mary Krozely, and Robert Oldham, reported in *The Journal of Consulting and Clinical Psychology*, showed similar findings with a group of fifty cancer patients. All of us wondered whether the imagery had any effect on helping the chemotherapy actually fight the cancer, but had no reliable way to tell.

The chemo staff allowed me to interview selected tape users so I could improve and more finely tune my imagery. This was very helpful. I learned, for instance, that many people winced at the sound of the phrase "natural killer cells," the medically correct term for some of the white blood cells that destroy cancer cells. To them, the imagery from those words was too jarringly murderous, impeding their concentration. So the term was deleted and "fighter cells" substituted. I learned that most patients welcomed imagery that was overtly spiritual, and some, in fact, wanted more than I had provided, so I retained some images that I worried some would find too religious-sounding. I learned that the music I had chosen annoyed some and made others too sleepy, so I changed it to a score with a little more instrumental texture, melody, and energy.

Soon I was making tapes for a variety of procedures and health conditions. The organ transplant support group that met at University Hospitals had an interest in using imagery to help combat organ rejection. The social work staff at the Cleveland Clinic wanted to learn how to use imagery to combat burnout. The local Mended Hearts group, an American Heart Association support group for people who have recovered from open-heart surgery, wanted to learn how to use imagery to lower blood pressure and reduce stress. I became a regular visitor to the American Cancer Society's "I Can Cope" support groups at several area hospitals, where patients wanted to learn how to use imagery for relaxation and to help contend with their illness. And so with the Cleveland chapters of the Multiple Sclerosis Society, the Lupus Foundation, and the local chapter of diabetes educators.

This meant I had to find willing tutors to teach me about different diseases and procedures, physicians and nurses who would be generous with their time and their knowledge. Fortunately, Cleveland is full of them. I also needed to investigate the research literature to see what kind of imagery was most effective and under what circumstances. New research findings were appearing every month, it seemed, and I was lucky enough to tap into a network of committed, excited investigators who were eager to share questions and answers. And, of course, most important, input from patients who were experiencing these diseases from the inside out humanized my findings and rounded out my education.

Because I couldn't begin to meet the demand for individual tapes, I made the decision to try and mass-produce them by illness category and procedure, thinking that at least they would be individualized and specific to that degree. Luck and good friends landed me on the doorstep of a creative, generous local businessman, George R. Klein, a distributor of books and magazines, who made the decision to capitalize this rather odd venture. Soon, we were producing a series of tapes, called *Health Journeys*, that consumers could purchase directly from drugstores and bookstores.

The tapes have been made available to various imagery research projects around the country. There are now several important ongoing investigations that we hope will help us fine-tune what we know and allow us to create better, more effective imagery. University Hospitals of Cleveland is studying the effects of imagery with HIV patients; Kaiser Permanente is looking at what imagery can do for surgery patients; and Sharp Memorial Hospital of San Diego is looking at the impact of imagery on heart patients. In fact, as I write this, it is clear to me that what we are learning about this field is growing so rapidly that this book will soon be in need of revision.

Every bit as precious as clinical research is the feedback we get from people from all over the country who have used guided imagery. Calls and letters have taught me this: Imagery helps a lot of people in dramatic ways. It reduces symptoms. It combats fear, isolation, depression, and anxiety. It engenders hope, optimism, and peace of mind. It combats illness. Although it doesn't work for everyone, it works for more people than we would think, and it isn't always predictable who that's going to be.

Even though most of my tapes were designed primarily for illnesses, like cancer, stroke, heart disease, M.S., rheumatoid arthritis, lupus, asthma, diabetes, and HIV infection, or for medical procedures, like surgery and chemotherapy, I found as I spoke to different groups that interest in simple wellness imagery was enormous. This interest was also reflected in the sales of the tapes: One imagery audiotape called *General Wellness*, which I recorded somewhat reluctantly, was hard to keep in stock.

People were eager to know how to use imagery to maintain their good health, reduce the effects of stress, and prevent problems before they began. And of course, this makes eminently good sense. Compared to the amount of work the body has to do to shrink a tumor or open a clogged artery, keeping itself well is a much simpler, easier, and more efficient expenditure of its effort.

I found that people wanted to know some basic guidelines, a reference book, a manual that taught the technique. Once informed by a solid knowledge base, they could then feel free to turn their imaginations loose on themselves in their own unique ways. With all I'd been taught by patients, workshop participants, health professionals, and researchers, I felt it was time to organize all the information I'd been given and get it down in a user-friendly book. So here it is.

This book organizes and explains current thinking about imagery, shows how and why it works, and under what conditions it works best. It also spells out eight different kinds of imagery that have been found to be effective, and offers samples of each kind in the form of imagery scripts or narratives. You can read these scripts to yourself, put them on audiotape, or have someone read them aloud to you.

These verbatim samples are what is called guided imagery, and they can be taken as a good place to start. They are tried-and-true and incorporate the elements needed for successful imagery that are described in earlier chapters of this book. What invariably happens, however, is that over time, with repetition, and sometimes even right away, the imagery becomes more and more spontaneous. The mind automatically starts to edit, consciously or unconsciously, adding meaningful associations and rich metaphors of its own. Of the scripted imagery, you will find that the images that have meaning to you will come to the fore, while those that are irrelevant fade into the background. Invariably, people report that although they started out conscientiously following a guided imagery tape or narrative, after regular use, at some point the content started shifting and changing, almost of its own accord. It's as if the unconscious mind knows what is needed and spontaneously provides it. It is this interplay between "programmed" imagery and "spontaneous" imagery that gets us in touch with the truth of our bodies and the deepest parts of ourselves.

I've organized this book so that Chapter 1 tells you what imagery is, why it works, and the circumstances that allow it to work best. Chapter 2 pulls together and describes all the different kinds of imagery that can be effective for health and well-being. Chapter 3 gives specific instructions on how to use imagery by yourself and provides several wellness imagery scripts to try, taken from the different categories put forth in Chapter 2. They are there for you to "mix and match" to suit yourself. My suggestion is that you make no assumptions about what will work and try them all—you may be surprised by what affects you most. Chapter 4 focuses on imagery for emotional wellness. Even though mental health is really not a separate issue, but part and parcel of general wellness, I gave it its own chapter because of its special interest to so many people. Imagery for common complaints, like headache, fatigue, insomnia, allergy, and pain, can be found in Chapter 5. And Chapter 6 answers the questions I'm most frequently asked about imagery. Resources are listed at the back.

I've tried to include good, real-life examples from my

practice, from the workshops I conduct, and from my personal life, to help keep the material alive and readily understandable. Besides, such stories are great motivators to give imagery a try. And who among us, after all, couldn't use a little more inspiration?

CHAPTER 1

HOW AND WHY IMAGERY WORKS

Images Are Events to the Body

Initially, most people make the mistake of thinking that imagery means something strictly visual. When I refer to imagery, I'm talking about *any perception that comes through any of the senses*. That means sights, sounds, smells, tastes, and feel. So, for instance, recalling the smell and feel of the air at the start of the first winter snowfall is an image. Remembering the sound and timbre of Daddy's smiling voice, saying he's proud of you, is an image. And recalling the internal bristle of energy in your body when you realize you are about to triumph at something you've been striving for—that it's going to happen—is also an image.

These sensory images are the true language of the body, the only language it understands immediately and without question. To the body, these images can be almost as real as actual events. This is the first operating principle of imagery: **Our bodies don't discriminate between sensory images in the mind and what we call reality.** Although images don't have the same intense impact on the body that real events do, they elicit the same essential quality of experience in the body. It's a little bit like what an echo is to the sound that generated it, or perhaps a pastel version of bold original colors. With a sensory image, echoes of the mood, emotions, physiological state, and blood chemistry associated with the original event reverberate in the body.

Now, this is a simple but profound fact. For instance, call to mind what happens to you when you read a recipe. Most likely, you start to salivate and feel hungrier. This is because, as you look over the recipe, your mind is creating images of how the food will look, smell, and taste, and perhaps even how the texture will feel in your mouth. Your body responds to the images, and, thinking that dinner is ready, happily prepares to eat by contracting your stomach muscles and producing extra saliva.

Sexual arousal often operates in the same way. The body is just as enthusiastic about sexual fantasy as reality, and sometimes more so. Here again, the body responds as if the images were actual events.

We see the downside of this principle when a grueling procedure such as chemotherapy is administered. Sometimes just the thought of returning for a treatment that, when last administered, induced nausea, vomiting, chills, sweats, and numbing fatigue is enough to reproduce those very same sensations in the car on the way to the hospital. Sometimes just the smell of the chemicals as the patient enters the treatment cubicle will get the whole reaction rolling again. Here, too, images imitate actual events.

The good news, of course, is that we can deliberately introduce healthful images, and the gullible body will respond as if they, too, were approximations of reality. A spate of research findings shows the physical changes that can occur in the body as a result of such engineering with the imagination.* A neuropsychologist at George Washington University Medical Center, Nicholas Hall, found that his subjects could use imagery to increase the number of circulating white blood cells, as well as levels of thymosin-alpha-1, a hormone used by T helper cells. So, too, Dr. Frank Lawlis and his team at the University of Texas found that imagery increased the numbers of neutrofils (debris ingester cells in the immune system) in the bloodstream. C. Wayne Smith and John Schneider at Michigan State University also showed that the imagination can affect the functioning of the neutrophils in very specific ways. Karen Olness, a physician at Rainbow Babies and Children's Hospital, University Hospitals of Cleveland, found that children were able to elevate their levels of immunoglobulin A, an indication of heightened immune function, in the saliva.

Other studies show the impact that imagery can have on allergic reactions. One remarkable study by Drs. Ikemi and Nakagawa at Yokohama City University School of Medicine in Japan showed that in 84 percent of their subjects, the use of imagery eliminated the standard histamine response to poison ivy—itching, redness, swelling, and blisters—when, under hypnosis, they imagined the poison ivy to be a harmless plant. Equally astonishing, the reverse

---

*When I refer to imagery, I am talking about imagery *in the altered state*—in other words, a form of self-hypnosis that uses for its content the deliberate production of healing sensory images. When you hear people distinguishing between imagery and hypnosis, claiming that hypnosis is effective while imagery is not, they are usually thinking of imagery as two-dimensional visualization in the normal, waking state. Admittedly, when defined in this way, imagery is usually not effective.

was also true: A large percentage of subjects broke out in a blistery rash when imagining a harmless plant to be poison ivy. Other studies show imagery to have a positive impact on depression, acne, and warts. One study even shows that imagery can result in breast enlargement.

Other research shows that imagery can help people in difficult and physically challenging circumstances. At the University of Texas Health Science Center in Dallas, Cornelia Kenner and Jeanne Achterberg showed that seriously injured burn patients who used imagery experienced less pain and used less pain medication; in another study, with people on the orthopedic unit who had multiple fractures, this same team showed that imagery significantly helped alleviate their pain and anxiety; D. H. Shuster at Iowa State University found that imagery reduced shock and increased blood flow in severely injured patients; I've already mentioned the team led by Jeanne Lyles at Vanderbilt University that showed that imagery reduced aversive responses to chemotherapy; and Carole Holden-Lund at Southeastern Louisiana University School of Nursing established that imagery lowers surgical stress and speeds up postsurgical wound healing. These findings are supported by two other more recent studies. Researchers from Papworth Hospital in Cambridge, England, found that patients who used guided imagery audiotapes during surgery recovered faster and left the hospital, on average, a day and a half earlier than other patients. And anesthesiologists Allen Hord and Peter Sebel and their colleagues at Emory University School of Medicine found that their sample of sixty patients who listened to guided imagery audiotapes during surgery required less morphine during their recovery than those who didn't. These latter studies point to the body's response to guided imagery even in the nonwaking state.

However compelling and fascinating these studies are, most of them are fairly short-term. They measure the immediate physical responses to imagery, limiting their scope to within days, hours, and sometimes only minutes of the intervention.

There is one study, however, by David Spiegal, a psychiatrist at Stanford University, that measures the effects years later. Spiegal divided a group of eighty-six middle-aged women with metastasized breast cancer into two groups. One group received state-of-the-art medical treatment only; the other received the same medical treatment, but along with it had weekly group counseling sessions for one year, where they learned self-hypnosis and guided imagery. The imagery was simple. They imagined themselves floating gently on water, feeling relaxed and peaceful. That was it.

As was expected, after the year was up, the second group reported less pain and discomfort, fewer mood swings, a generally more optimistic outlook, and a greater feeling of being in control. This in and of itself was no big surprise. Social scientists have known since World War II that social support and group cohesion will help people with their attitudes and emotional resiliency. But ten years later, curious about long-term effects, Spiegal decided to check the death records of all eighty-six patients. Much to his surprise, he found that the second group had lived an average of twice as long as the first (36.6 months versus 18.9 months). Here was evidence that the effects of either group support or imagery or both didn't stop at psychological implications, but showed up in profound, lasting physiological results.

So images in the mind are real events to the body. Perhaps you can remember, for instance, what it felt like to be read to by Gramma when you were little: the delicious warmth of sitting in her soft, warm lap, the feel of her favorite old sweater and the scent of her soap, the sound of her low, loving voice, saying the same words for the hundredth time, leaning so close to you that her breath tickled your ear. And perhaps, too, you can remember the blissful feeling of being prized and precious, safe and protected, that came from sitting there. That memory is a real event to the body. As far as your body is concerned, regardless of intervening years, age, or pounds, while you're remembering all that rich, sensory detail, you're *still* on Gramma's lap.

And whatever profound emotional nourishment you got there is yours to have again. Whatever neurohormones, or chemical messengers, went coursing through your bloodstream as you sat on Gramma's lap, sending happy-to-be-alive white blood cells all through your body, these same substances get activated again. As far as your body is concerned, Gramma is forever available to love and sustain you.

And so with any sweet memories: a wonderful vacation; a perfect moment, either alone in nature or with someone else; a time when you felt filled with purpose or madly in love; or a time of great triumph. As long as it is *grounded in sensory memory*, the language of the body, you can revisit that moment over and over, each time taking from it all the richness and nourishment it has to give you.

The Power of the Altered State

The second key principle that makes guided imagery work is this: **In the altered state, we are capable of more rapid and intense healing, growth, learning,**

and change. This is another one of those profound but simple truths that we have all experienced.

By altered state, I mean a state of relaxed focus, a kind of calm but energized alertness, a focused reverie. Attention is concentrated on one thing, or on a very narrow band of things. As this happens, we find we have a heightened sensitivity to what we are focused on, and a decreased awareness of the other things going on around us, things we would ordinarily notice. We are all familiar with this state. We're in it when we're so engrossed that we lose track of time; we don't hear people talking to us.

In practical terms, this kind of altered-state experience allows us to reach peak performance levels in many areas of endeavor. There is a kind of self-forgetfulness and disregard for outcome that characterizes this state, allowing us to outreach what we thought we could do. This state is sometimes called "flow" or being "in the zone." In it, artists and athletes can extend their normal range of achievement. Proposal writers can propose better; rescuers can rescue better; charmers can charm better. Indeed, if you check out the close-ups on your TV of the face of your favorite quarterback having a good day, what you'll see is the relaxed, glowing, focused look of the altered state.

We are in and out of altered states all day long. Sometimes it's just for a matter of seconds. It happens, for instance, when we're in a crowded elevator, and strangers are uncomfortably close to us, invading physical space that is normally reserved for intimate relationships. Our defense is to stare straight ahead, concentrating on an imaginary spot on the elevator door or on the lit floor indicator above the door, blocking out our perceptions of the people breathing down our necks. Often, even in the few seconds it takes to get to the twelfth floor, we've lost track of time, and we experience a mini-jolt when we hear the *ding* that signifies we've arrived.

The altered state also demonstrates its remarkable but everyday power at the times when we wake up from sleep with a crystal-clear solution to a niggling problem that's been dogging us for weeks. Sometimes it's a new perspective or insight; sometimes it's a mysterious shift in attitude. When this happens, the magical altered state of sleep, dreams, and half-awake reverie has been at work for us, in wonderful ways we still don't altogether understand.

This state also works for us during times of extreme trauma and extraordinary stress. Someone experiencing an assault or a car wreck becomes hyperalert, perceiving everything in slow motion, as the mind and body organize for survival by picking up every possible detail, every minute cue available. This intense alertness in the altered state is often what saves us, because in it we can respond to the situation with speed, efficiency, and clarity. However, as many trauma survivors know all too well, long after the danger has passed, it is not so easy to put aside these memories. They've been seared into the brain in the potent altered state.

Because of renewed interest in the value of altered states of consciousness, the fields of psychotherapy, education, and health are all undergoing major innovations and exciting changes. Stanislav Grof, a psychiatrist who developed a technique called holotropic breathwork, uses intense, deep breathing to induce the altered state. By working with the images and body sensations that come up in this state, he is able to help people make psychological breakthroughs that normally would take months of psychotherapy to achieve. In fact, some of his results probably would not occur in standard, verbal psychotherapy.

I've been at hypnosis training sessions where we were able, in the altered state, to control our heart rate, musculature, and other body functions well beyond the so-called normal range. In one such workshop, four plucky volunteers were stuck with a sterile needle through a large vein in the top of the hand. They had decided ahead of time whether or not they wanted to bleed when the needle was pulled out, and if so, whether they wanted to bleed from one or both of the resulting punctures. In the altered state, their bodies did exactly as they were bidden. One person bled not at all; two bled from one of the punctures; and one bled from both. This particular workshop was not for the faint at heart.

I've also participated in a standard Ericksonian induction technique,★ where the task was to pay attention to three instructors talking to us at the same time. My overloaded brain promptly went into the altered state, because that is the only way I and most human beings can follow three verbal deliveries at once.

My college roommate was her psychology instructor's subject for several classroom hypnosis experiments. The professor expressed her gratitude to Ellen by allowing her to study for her exams in the altered state. Ellen would thus have perfect visual recall during exams. She was able to leaf through pages in her head, "reading" whole paragraphs. Ellen, who was admittedly a very good student anyway, never had an easier time with recall.

So that is the second operating principle of guided imagery: In the altered state, our capacity for any number of things is vastly enhanced.

★Milton Erickson, a psychiatrist, was a brilliant, groundbreaking hypnotherapist who developed a method of working with people in the altered state that is followed today by many practitioners.

The Importance of Feeling in Charge

Using a technique like imagery—something that is entirely within our control, for use when, how, and where we want—is, in and of itself, beneficial. It has the benign, placebo effect of making us the "locus of control," as they say in social science talk. And this brings me to the third and final principle that operates with guided imagery and its effectiveness: **We feel better about ourselves when we have a sense of mastery over what is happening to us.** Conversely, a sense of helplessness lowers self-esteem, not to mention our ability to cope and our hopefulness about the future.

A sense of mastery was of utmost importance to Sally. I remember when she first came to see me, a tall, beautiful, athletic young homemaker and mother, who had recently been diagnosed with multiple sclerosis. Normally calm and self-possessed, Sally was in near-hysteria. In fact, she'd created quite a ruckus at the hospital, which was why they'd promptly referred her for psychotherapy. What had nearly sent her 'round the bend was her ambiguous prognosis. She'd been told that she had a disease that could go into remission, or could get a lot worse, either sooner or later, and that there was not a whole lot she could do about it except get tested at regular intervals, and wait and see.

When we started discussing some of the things Sally could do on her own with imagery, she immediately became calm. In fact, her mood got very focused, energized, and, believe it or not, even a little euphoric. Because here was something she could actually *do* to help herself. She immediately went into her "achieving jock" mode and put her considerable drive and talent into developing this new skill of imaging. As with everything else Sally did, she became a champion at it. Now, several years and two additional pregnancies later, she is doing very well. In fact, her doctors are saying they are no longer sure she has M.S. But that is another story, a very complex one without clear answers. The point I want to make here is that just having a technique that she could use at her discretion gave Sally back her sense of control and personal effectiveness and did her mental health a world of good, regardless of the outcome.

Some of the earliest social science research establishes that when we have a sense of mastery over our lives, we feel better and do better. One study of people who reported a reluctance to fly found that it was not a fear of flying per se, but a fear of *being flown by somebody else*. The reluctance disappeared with the notion that they could have the role of pilot and be in charge.

A study of noise stress showed that people were jarred and disturbed by the sound of nearby trains rumbling through their neighborhoods only when it happened at random or unexpected times. When the trains were expected, people felt in control and were able to adjust to them. In fact, they barely *heard* the expected trains. But unscheduled trains were upsetting and noisy to them.

Numerous studies of work environments, starting with the famous Western Electric studies, show that when workers feel they have some say about their jobs, their productivity improves and there is a decrease in on-the-job accidents and absenteeism. Researcher Robert Karasek, in studying high rates of heart disease at Cornell University Medical College, found that "job strain" for most people was a matter of feeling little or no control over the varying demands of the job. These were the people most likely to have elevated blood pressure and heart problems.

We know from our own experience that when we feel some control over what is happening to us, we feel more confidence and optimism. I remember when, as a young mother, I learned that my three-year-old daughter, who had been waking up with stiff, swollen, painful joints, probably had rheumatoid arthritis. I was as upset as I've ever been. I remember thinking that nothing would ever be the same, for her or for me, and that there was nothing anyone could say or do to make me feel better.

After several weeks of feeling quite devastated, I was told by a friend that she admired how I was handling the situation. She thought I was doing a good job of helping my daughter without turning her into an invalid. I was astonished at how much this feedback lifted my spirits. The situation hadn't changed. My daughter was still sick. Yet, somehow I felt dramatically better about everything, simply for having been told I was doing a good job at controlling what I could. A lot of my energy returned; so did my optimism and hope about her future. That year I learned a lot about the positive impact of a sense of mastery, in a very personal way.

So if we combine these three operating principles by (1) introducing images to the mind that the body believes are actual events, and (2) doing this in the altered state, and (3) doing it when, how, and where we want to, we have at our command the unique, powerful, and versatile technique of guided imagery.

Some Things That Make Imagery More Effective

PRACTICE

Skill at using imagery increases with practice. Don't worry if your first attempts don't seem effective. Just as with exercising any muscle, your capacity grows over time with use. The more you use imagery, the more your response to it deepens, intensifies, and becomes more controllable. So don't make limiting assumptions about your capacity. It will grow exponentially.

Some people are "naturals" at imagery. With no apparent effort, they can launch themselves into full, rich, vivid reverie. Others will start off insisting that they don't "see things." But they are wrong. Everyone "sees things." We all imagine and fantasize, even if it's just a matter of thinking about what we should have said to the boss in that last irritatingly unsatisfactory encounter. Possibly, people who think they can't imagine are using the wrong senses to get started. Some of us are much more auditory or tactile than visual; others of us are more responsive to taste and smell. All that's required is a willingness to experiment to see which sensory avenue works best, followed by time and practice.

By practice, I usually mean in five-to-twenty-minute blocks of time, depending on your capacity for sustained concentration, one or two times a day, for at least two or three weeks, and possibly as part of a permanent daily routine. The powerful, dreamy periods when we're waking up in the morning and falling asleep at night are good times to do this. What you'll find if you get into the habit of using imagery is that you will become more and more efficient, until you are able to access deep, intense images in a matter of seconds. The payoff comes when you are stopped at a red light and, rather than feeling annoyed by the delay, you find yourself using the time to lower your blood pressure.

Another reason people might have initial trouble is a difficulty with sustained concentration. This, too, improves dramatically with practice. Unfortunately, some of us have become so scattered and distracted that it takes us a while to focus our attention on one thing and leave it there. But keep in mind, this is a skill we all once had. Watch the single-minded absorption of a baby checking out its toes and you will see the kind of sustained attention you once could hold. It can be regained easily with simple practice, and you have the added benefit of improving concentration in other areas of your life.

More difficult to change is the kind of edgy skit-tishness that some of us have about being physically still. Some people have a patterned inability to settle down. They tend to focus on external things, stay busy, and resist focusing inward. It can be a kind of permanent anxiety state, being continually spring-loaded to respond to *something*—some emergency, difficulty, or demand, coming from somewhere. This makes it initially hard to engage in the quiet, internal work of imagery. And of course, these are the people who could use it the most.

Physiologists like Dr. Barbara Brown, who did groundbreaking work with biofeedback at the Veterans Administration Hospital in Sepulveda, California, explain to us that this hypervigilance was functional back in the days of the saber-toothed tiger, when, if we didn't move fast, we became dinner. And in those days, our physical response—running away, tossing spears, or climbing trees—used up all the adrenaline that mobilized us in the first place. So we got tired but calm again. The system worked well back then. Unfortunately, our physiological evolution hasn't caught up with modern times.

Our lives now don't afford us with the systematic opportunity to dissipate adrenaline. Nowadays, it's almost always some psychosocial event that stresses us, not physi-cal danger, and the adrenaline stays overlong in the bloodstream, rendering us edgy and irritable. For some of us, this becomes a way of life.

People with this difficulty get annoyed and upset when they try to be still; relaxing is experienced as alarming to the body, which at some level is saying, "Are you kidding? We gotta get out of here!" It is sometimes helpful for people with this problem to attempt their imaging while engaged in a mild, rote form of physical exercise, such as walking.

ALLOWING VS. FORCING

Imagery works best in a permissive, unforced atmosphere. It is a gentle, amorphous, right-brain activity that thrives on a soft, receptive state of mind. Commanding, scolding, or threatening yourself not only won't work but will probably defeat your purpose. There's nothing quite like a harsh, authoritative, pointing finger, even your own, for pulling you out of the sweet territory of healing dreams.

What seems to work best with imagery is an attitude of *allowing*, with respect for your own autonomy and need for choices. In a sense, you are asking permission of yourself to clear away space so your images can appear. If you find that you are in a fruitless power struggle with yourself, trying to "make" yourself have this experience, the best thing to do is to just let it go and attend to something else for a while.

Sometimes you will want to very deliberately introduce specific images, designed to orchestrate certain events in your mind and body. At other times you will be interested to see what images spontaneously arise. At those times when you're trying to orchestrate specific images, you may find that you're getting no cooperation whatso-ever; that even though you keep putting forth an image that you think is appropriate, your deep self just isn't hav-ing any of it, and the image won't "take." This is when it is best to be flexible. Set aside your agenda and ask for *what wants to be there* instead. (This passive language is deliberate. The clearest, truest images show up when we take this receptive attitude and just allow the images to come, as if they had a life of their own. They do.) Then let yourself be surprised.

Usually, over time and with practice, your experi-ences with imagery become a kind of dialogue between both kinds of images, the deliberate ones and the spontane-ous ones. A kind of continuing movie evolves, with sur-prising twists and turns, once you put yourself in this receptive mode and let the images roll.

Do keep in mind that your imagery is not going to look like a clearly defined Technicolor movie. As I've al-ready mentioned, it's more likely to be a multisensory hodgepodge, amorphous, and wavering in intensity. So please don't expect your imagery to come up to Holly-wood production standards.

Nor do old notions of "paying attention" apply here. This is the sort of experience where it is normal to fade in and out. So don't expect the kind of rigorous, alert attentiveness that you invoked to, say, study for exams. That was using the left side of your brain. This is your right side. The right brain is dreamy, nonlogical, and laid-back.

If you find yourself persisting in bossing, critiquing, and reprimanding yourself, try to do what a participant in a workshop once suggested: Create the image of putting all your self-criticisms, kicking and screaming, on a raft and floating them gently downstream.

STICKING TO YOUR VALUES

Imagery also works best when the imagery you choose feels right to you, when it's congruent with who you are and how you walk in the world. You may not feel comfortable with the warlike imagery of natural killer cells annihilating bacteria in your body; you may prefer to focus on other aspects of your immune system, such as the microphages munching on debris. Some people prefer to focus on the defensive nature of the immune system, because only *justified* aggression feels acceptable to them.

Several years ago, a dear friend of mine, Wil Garcia, who had AIDS, was encouraged to imagine his T cells wreaking havoc with the virus in his body. Back in those days, this was thought to be the only "correct" imagery for cancer and HIV. But Wil was such a genuinely gentle, *un*warlike person, he just couldn't picture his white blood cells attacking, poisoning, and chomping his virus to death. It just wasn't *him*.

Instead, he came up with imagery that was more congruent with who he was. In the receptive, open state I described earlier, he conjured up a magical, pink, gooey substance, a lot like Pepto-Bismol, that coated the virus from stem to stern, as he reassured it in his gentle, caring way that it was in a good, safe environment where no one would hurt it, and it could therefore feel free to just go back to sleep.

Wil went from having full-blown AIDS, complete with Kaposi's sarcoma, to being symptom-free for about three years. At the time, no one thought that was possible. But his virus did in fact go back to sleep. And he wasn't on any medication at the time. When he did die three years later, it was from an intestinal virus. He suffered with it for only four or five weeks.

Interestingly enough, subsequent research has shown that when the HIV is coated with protein in a test tube, it cannot be absorbed by the T cell and begin its cycle of damage. Wil's intuitive imagery was accurate, even though he had no way of knowing it at the time. To him, it just felt right.

There are many ways to make imagery congruent. I've seen people with a tremendous interest in cooking use culinary metaphors in their imagery. One woman with fibroid tumors imagined that her uterus held plums that dried into prunes and then shriveled into dust. Bonnie, my assertive friend on chemotherapy, had a strong attachment to the idea of her mother taking care of her, and also found cleanliness very attractive. As a result, she had her mother scrubbing, vacuuming, and scouring her cancer cells away. Another woman, a classical musician whose favorite author was J. R. R. Tolkien, had hobbits chasing a cleansing river of magical healing all through her body, to the chords of Wagner's "Ride of the Valkyries" crashing in her ears from her headset.

THE POWER OF THE GROUP

Most people are able to respond better to a guided imagery narration, from either a speaker or an audiotape, when in a group as opposed to being alone. The altered state is contagious. When people are surrounded by others in a deep reverie, they are more likely to get into one themselves. It seems that we can access these states by virtue of sheer proximity. Those who study consciousness call this direct induction or entrainment. It is as if we are able to hitch a ride on someone else's powerful brain waves, and so go farther faster.

In practical terms, this means that if you're having difficulty getting into your imagery by yourself, you can go to a guided imagery workshop or class, experience imagery with a whole group, and get a permanent, residual boost. Most people report that their imagery is more vivid, intense, and powerful in a group and that the effects will then stay with them in subsequent sessions by themselves.

During group exercises in my workshops, many veteran imagers will report something new happening for them—some surprising bonus popping up from the unconscious, a powerful revelation from the deep self. Some report that a familiar imaging experience will have more powerful emotion attached to it. It is intriguing that once this level is achieved in a group, it can then be repeated alone. It is as if a new route is carved out in the brain and can then be traveled in subsequent sessions with ease. When I hear people say they have difficulty meditating alone and need to meet with their group, I think they are referring to this phenomenon (aside from the usual social support considerations)—the contagious nature of the altered state.*

PLAYING MUSIC

Listening to music while practicing guided imagery is another factor that can increase its effectiveness. Many

---

*If you have an interest in understanding the physics of this phenomenon, the best explanation I've ever found is in the book *Stalking the Wild Pendulum*, by Itzhak Bentov. In it, he explains that this contagiousness of consciousness is much like putting together several grandfather clocks in the same room. Even though at first their pendulums will all be swinging at different intervals, over time they will start to synchronize, and the tick-tocks will become uniform. So, too, with the brain waves of the altered state. Subatomic physics teaches us that we humans are ultimately composed of vibration, even though we are cleverly disguised as solid matter. When we look closely (subatomically), we find we are mere *fluctuations of energy*, and, just like those grandfather clocks, we'll all start pulsating in sync with the most powerful vibration, in one unified field.

things are apprehended on the right side of the brain, the part of the mind that engages in the altered state. Some of these things are the processing of sensory information, images, humor, emotion, and music. But because either music or imagery alone can induce the altered state, the two in combination are powerfully synergistic.

I've had many people tell me that they are deeply affected by music. Some say it's the most powerful mood-altering experience they've ever had. If this is the case for you, it may be that music alone is enough for you to use to create your own spontaneous images; and possibly a guided imagery tape that has someone speaking on it, even if it's you, would be a distraction and a hindrance. In this case, I would recommend that you try out several kinds of music, to see what suits you best. Again, leave room to be surprised. You may find that music you don't even particularly like elicits powerful, healing imagery for you.

It is certainly true that words are much more confining and limiting than images by themselves. The minute we try to cram what we perceive into the artificial constraints of language, we've already tampered with the truth and limited it to some degree. So if you are strongly affected by music, you may want to see what comes up for you, using only your own choice of music as background, un-contaminated by words.

Ironically enough, the people that I've found to have the most difficulty using music are the "serious" musicians: those who study it, play it for a living, or in some other way analyze and evaluate it on a regular basis. Many of these folks can't help but have their critic-judger, that great, left-brain killer of the reverie state, butt in at the sound of the first musical phrase. So much for sweet dreams. If this is what happens with you, you're better off without music for accompaniment.

There are now experts in the rapidly emerging field of music therapy who say that there are some reliable rules of thumb about what kinds of music to choose for what kinds of imagery. For instance, if you want music to help you with anxiety, tension, high blood pressure, or a fast pulse rate, you are encouraged to listen to music with a beat that's slower than your heart rate (under seventy-two beats per minute). This "entrains" the pulse to slow down and match the beat of the music, just like those pendulums in the grandfather clocks of Bentov's experiment. You might also want a melody that is slow and sustained, with smooth, flowing phrasing, and with softer quality instruments, like flute, oboe, strings, and voice. Most versions of Pachelbel's *Canon* fill this bill. So does the adagietto from Mahler's Fifth Symphony or the Barber *Adagio for Strings*. Mike Rowland's *Fairy Ring* is a lovely popular piece that works well. These are just suggestions. Don't let them preclude your own preferences.

On the other hand, if you need to have your spirits lifted and an infusion of energy to counter fatigue or depression, or to jolt a weary immune system back into action, you might prefer a beat that is above heart rate (seventy-two to ninety-two beats per minute), with minimal reverberation and an inspiring, emotive melody. Some classical pieces that provide this combination are the last movement of Beethoven's Fifth or Ninth Symphony and the finale of Mahler's Fifth. Popular works are *Prelude to Lazarus* and much of the sound track from the movies *Superman* and *Silverado*.

But beware of all these rules and suggestions. Your own intuitive reaction will very likely tell you all you need to know. When the first musician I collaborated with to score my tapes got overly caught up in these criteria for "correct" healing music, his music became flat and lifeless.

It wasn't the way he worked best. Fortunately, he went back to his old way of composing and managed to create music that was beautiful, yet at the same time intuitively met these requirements. So listen to what feels right and good for you. You'll—forgive the pun—know the score.

THE EMOTIONAL CONNECTION

Alongside music and sensory information, emotions also comfortably coexist with imagery on the right side of the brain. Because of this neighborly connection, imagery that elicits emotion is powerful imagery. I frequently present this material at workshops and self-help groups, guiding people in many kinds of imagery exercises. When I see a face that is rapt with joy or touched by tears, I know that important work is going on, even if I have no idea what it's about. And, sure enough, during the break, the person will often come up to me and confide that something intense, powerful, and transformative has happened.

Many people are surprised by the tears that will start to flow during a benign, introductory imagery exercise. I will sometimes lead a group in a very simple guided meditation, where they go to a favorite place, see it in all its rich sensory detail, and feel a sense of internal peace and gratitude for being there. This will often generate quiet tears. Sometimes people will even ask why they were sad. Of course, in this case, they weren't. Emotions of love and gratitude generate tears just as readily as sadness does, and many people mistake being touched for feeling sad. At other times, it's an old well of sorrow or nostalgia that has come bubbling up to the surface. In the altered state, the heart opens wide and any emotion intensifies. Generally, people who aren't familiar with their feelings might have trouble identifying the subtler variations in their emotions for a while.

Practice changes that. The more we experience imagery, the more conversive we become with our feelings. Our emotions become far more available to us, both in the normal, waking state and in subsequent imagery experiences. And the more our emotions are available to us, the more vivid and powerful our imagery gets. And there's another major benefit: Becoming more in tune with our feelings is good for our mental health and emotional resiliency, even when it initially feels uncomfortable. Mental health experts studying David Spiegal's research at Stanford wonder if the group of breast cancer patients who lived twice as long did so not so much from guided imagery or from the emotional support of the group experience, but from just *expressing their feelings* more.* Subsequent research by Fawzy I. Fawzy and his colleagues at the UCLA Neuropsychiatric Institute also points to emotional expression being a major factor in producing positive changes in immune functioning for up to six months after their six-week education/support group experiment. Future research might sort all this out. I think all three factors played an important part.

Of course, it's not always sweetness and light that one feels during an imaging experience. Some kinds of imagery, for instance, are deliberately designed by therapists to help a person relive a trauma so they can at last gain some mastery over it. These past experiences can otherwise continue to plague them and diminish their capacity to live their lives fully. In the altered state, they will

---

*Researchers who investigate neuropeptides and cell behavior are now suspecting that experiencing *any* emotion, regardless of how unpleasant, is essentially healthful. It is when we wall ourselves off from emotion, deny our feelings, and experience their absence that we run into trouble.

feel again all the fear, rage, and confusion that they felt at the time of the trauma, only this time it is in the trustworthy company of a trained professional, who can also use imagery to help them heal the wounds once they are reexperienced. (It is also true that in the altered state, while part of the person is reliving the trauma, another part—the current adult in the present reality—is detached, safe, and watching. This "split consciousness" that we can achieve during the altered state is what makes the experience bearable.)

It is the power of these authentic emotions that the imagery elicits, emotions that sometimes have no conscious memory in the normal, waking state, that opens the door for healing. And because images are experienced by the body as real events, we *can*, over time, transform our self-perception from victim to survivor.

THE MAGIC OF TOUCH

Touch is possibly the most powerful accompaniment for increasing the effects of imagery. It settles down the most jittery of listeners, so they can avail themselves of its benefits; and it also makes the images themselves far more vivid, intense, and emotionally present than they might otherwise be. Most of us are deeply affected by touch.

Imagery has come a long way from the days of the initial pioneering work of O. Carl Simonton, M.D., a radiotherapist, and his former wife, Stephanie Matthews-Simonton, who were the first real pioneers in developing imagery for cancer patients and in studying its impact. They encouraged their subjects, cancer patients with advanced disease, to relax and visualize their immune systems attacking their cancer in symbolic form: for instance, seeing powerful sharks encircling skinny, frightened fish, or noble armies of strong, valiant knights vanquishing a ragtag band of ruffians. Although their initial impressions were very promising, they have not been replicated by subsequent research. Some attribute those first results to the placebo effect of the researchers' early excitement washing over onto their patients. Certainly, enthusiasm and hope are powerful and contagious enough to happily confound research outcomes.

But since those early days, we've all learned a lot more about imagery. We know now that it needs to be a multisensory experience, accessed in the altered state, and probably most effective when felt as sensation in the body. In the sixties and seventies, imagery was something essentially visual and two-dimensional. Imagery meant flat, disembodied pictures produced in the head. One problem with this view was that people who weren't particularly "visual" didn't do well with it; those with auditory and kinesthetic imaginations, for example, were at a disadvantage. Secondly, for physical and emotional well-being, imagery needs to be experienced *in the body* for maximum impact. This was the lesson that Elmer and Alyce Green, two tireless biofeedback pioneers from the Menninger Foundation, and their gifted psychologist daughter, Patricia Norris, taught us.

Biofeedback uses electronic equipment to measure subtle changes in the body, such as brain waves or galvanic skin response, by way of sensors attached to the scalp or fingertips. The machine then signals the information with a sound tone, light, or picture on a screen. With this kind of instantaneous feedback about their tension level, pulse rate, blood pressure, and so on, people become highly attuned to their own bodies and can identify internal sensation as never before. And with this kind of sensitive attunement to the body comes control of these supposedly autonomic functions, just as those oft-cited yogis from India are able to do. Thus, a man with hypertension can imagine his blood moving in a slow, steady fashion through wide, smooth, supple arteries, and the machinery will tell him when he's on the mark and actually lowering his blood pressure. After some practice, he can operate effectively without the machine and know what his blood pressure is and how to adjust it on his own. The work of the Greens, combining imagery with biofeedback, provided an essential missing piece: the importance of focusing on how the body feels; the value of kinesthetic imagery.

In addition, the emerging practice of therapeutic massage was coming up with the same conclusions, but from the opposite direction. As massotherapists from many differing training specialties worked on problematic backs, necks, hips, and shoulders, some of their patients reported vivid imagery popping into their consciousness. It was as if the images were lodged in the tissue and turned loose and brought to light by the touch of the therapist. Some of the images were abstract, some symbolic, and some were very clearly memories of long-forgotten events. To better deal with this material from the psyche, many professional body workers felt pressed either to pursue further psychological training for themselves or to develop collaborative relationships with psychotherapists. A powerful connection was becoming apparent: Clearly, imagery was fused with muscle, skin, and bone.

So, too, psychotherapy was embracing the idea that images and the body were inescapably intertwined. Holistic Gestalt and Jungian ideas were gaining prominence, extending traditional thinking beyond the simplistic cause-and-effect tenets of psychoanalysis and psychosomatic medicine (areas of study that, interestingly enough, are both rapidly going out of favor) to something much more profoundly integrated: that images are an expression of the body, and the body is the concrete expression of its images. They were beginning to be seen as inseparable, part and parcel of the same thing.

From all these differing perspectives, the bottom line was the same for the clinical practice of imagery: Multisensory, kinesthetic imagery was far more effective for healing than the flat, strictly visual, two-dimensional variety. And because of this, breath, movement, and touch became the keys for unlocking the power of sensory imagery.

Most people can, in fact, imagine things happening *inside* their bodies. This is effective imagery. A good, standard exercise might be to have someone focus his or her attention on the breath, imagining that with each inhale, the warm energy of the breath is going to tight, tense places, warming, massaging, and loosening them, and then releasing the unwanted discomfort with the exhale. Adult-onset diabetics can put their hands over the midriff as they imagine their insulin moving out of the pancreas to connect with hungry cells throughout the body; asthmatics can put their hands on the chest as they sense the airways of the lungs opening and clearing. Touch used in this way helps direct awareness to the appropriate places inside the body, while making the imagery more intense and powerful at the same time.

So, putting your hand over your heart and imagining a calm, loving reassurance coming out of the warmth of your hand and into your chest, suggesting that your heart needn't be in such a hurry, will very likely slow the pulse down to a nice, calm, steady beat. The body is readily persuaded by touch and is inclined to believe a kind hand on it. And by focusing on the sensation of peacefulness coming *into* your chest, you are automatically locating your consciousness inside your body, the most centered and grounded place it can be.

I remember one man who came with his wife to an "I Can Cope" cancer support group session I was conducting at a local hospital. He was in a wheelchair and had oxygen tubes down his nose. He was physically uncomfortable and chronically anxious. Tumors in his lungs had left him short of breath, rendering him unable to take the standard deep, relaxing breaths that set the stage for most of the imagery we'd been doing. (Because anxiety alone makes us breathe rapidly and shallowly, we will automatically feel anxious when short of breath, just by association.) He was very unhappy, restless, and anxious, and couldn't settle into the different imagery exercises the group was doing, until we came to one that made use of touch.

I had his wife stand behind him, put her hands on his shoulders, and imagine that all the love and concern that she had for him was moving from the warmth of her heart into her hands and into his shoulders. The man was free to imagine that the warmth from her hands was going to anyplace in his body that needed it, to soothe and comfort him.

At the end of the exercise, the man and his wife were both softly crying. He said this was the first moment's peace he'd had in over a year. His constant fear, agitation, and physical discomfort had been dissipated by something as simple as his wife's touch. He wept with relief. His wife wept, too, with gratitude for having something she could do to help him.

This example—a common one, I might add—raises the related issue of *jointly sharing* touch and imagery with someone else, as a way of increasing the effectiveness of the imagery. My experience is that sharing a joint image can be very helpful and increases the intensity of the images. It also gives two people a structured but tender way to be with one another. As with the man's wife in the group, it can provide a satisfying means of helping someone you love.

When my daughter was twelve, she broke her shoulder and had to have it wrapped in a sling under her clothes. Like any twelve-year-old, she was exquisitely self-conscious and hated the way she looked with her new, bulky profile. In her desperation, she was even willing to try some of her mother's strange methods, if it would get her looking "normal" faster. So together we discussed how bones heal. We looked carefully at the X ray of her break. We also checked out pictures from my reference books of how cells mobilize to repair bone tissue. And then, together, we snuggled up and imagined her fractured bone knitting back together, while she placed her hand over the break and sensed "healing energy" (her words, not mine) entering the bone and speeding up the process. I put my hand over hers and imagined the same thing. Most of this was done silently, but occasionally I would remind her aloud of some of the images: the extra blood traveling to the site to speed healing (could she feel the warmth of it?); the broken edges of the bone interweaving with the help of fresh, new cells, acting like cement (did it maybe even itch a little, the way new tissue growth sometimes does?); the vigilant white blood cells on patrol, keeping infection away (could she feel the buzz of all that activity?); and the surrounding muscle staying vital, firm, and strong, in spite of its impaired mobility.

We did this two or three times a day, about ten minutes each time. Each of us enjoyed the intimacy of those little imagery sessions, so if there were no other benefits, we got to have some very special time together. But after three weeks, her arm had healed, *three weeks earlier* than her orthopedist had predicted. Now, I can't prove that our two imaginations worked better than one. Nor can I prove that using touch made the imagery work better. I can't even prove that using imagery of any kind whatsoever accelerated the knitting of her bones. It's possible that she was just a speedy mender. But in my heart I feel quite satisfied that all of those things did help.

I haven't included any discussion of the energetic nature of touch here. This is such a profound, complex, and complicated area, so deeply interwoven with the very nature of imagery, that I've saved it for Chapter 2.

DIFFERENT KINDS
OF IMAGERY

There are many kinds of imagery that work well. There is imagery that focuses on what is happening microscopically *in the cells*; physical imagery at the observable, *physiological* level; *metaphoric imagery*, the imagery that plays with the symbols of what's happening physically or psychologically; *psychological imagery*, which is imagery that changes a person's way of looking at him- or herself; *spiritual imagery*, which focuses on the vaster, nonordinary dimensions of reality; *end-state imagery*, which highlights the concrete, short-term goals we are striving for; *feeling-state imagery*, imagery that aims toward changing mood or emotional tone in a very broad way; and *energetic imagery*, imagery that uses the physics of our electromagnetic field as its focus.

In this chapter, I'll be describing each of these types of imagery so you can get a general sense of what might appeal to you for your own personal use. Later on, in Chapter 3, you'll find specific script samples for each of these categories, along with specific suggestions about where, when, and how to use them. But for now, just look over the different kinds and get a preliminary sense of the range of possibilities that are open to you. Some will appeal to you more than others. And you may find that your preferences change over time. But this will give you an overview and a place to start.

None of these categories are absolutely distinct from each other. For instance, often psychological imagery will be metaphoric in nature, with a physiological component that is part and parcel of it. The distinctions I make here are mainly so I can show you each kind, simply and clearly.

FEELING-STATE IMAGERY

Probably the most basic form of imagery is the kind geared to simply change your mood. I call this feeling-state imagery, and it doesn't require sophisticated knowledge of the mind or the body. Anyone can do it, and in spite of its simplicity, it can produce some pretty impressive results with your general health and well-being.

It was this kind of simple, mood-shifting imagery that David Spiegal used in the Stanford cancer study: Subjects imagined themselves floating very gently on water, feeling peaceful and relaxed. This was the content of the self-hypnosis exercise, given over and over again in the support groups and used by the women as needed outside of them. This simple image helped these anxious, frightened patients in the advanced stages of metastasized breast cancer to feel more calm and in control.

Another example of this kind of imagery is when you let your imagination take you to your favorite place, any special retreat of yours, real or imagined, and call to mind what it's like to be there with all of your senses; or reliving an especially sweet encounter or nourishing moment, remembering the feelings that filled you then. It's astonishing how quickly we can move from a feeling state of tension and fear to one of peace and calm.

Imagery can also help us shift to a state of optimism, generosity, confidence, and courage. Perhaps some high-energy expansiveness is required of us, and we don't feel we have it to summon up. Rather than "fake it" with inauthentic bravado, which rarely fools anyone anyway, we can use mood-altering imagery to genuinely open ourselves up.

One client of mine, Harriet, could sing like an angel, but was so beleaguered by stage fright and performance anxiety that she shrank from auditioning for soloist roles, even though in her heart she knew that those soprano pieces had her name on them. Her fear would close up her throat and distort the beauty of her voice. With an audition looming on the horizon, we decided to try an imagery experiment to fortify her for it. After coaching her to use her breathing to help her relax, I encouraged her to remember, with all the sensory detail she could muster, a time when she sang unencumbered and her voice just soared. Where was she? What did the room look and feel like? Who else was there? What did they look like? What did her body feel like? Could she hear herself? With each answer to each question, Harriet more and more intensely experienced the expansiveness and joy that she felt at that time.

Harriet visibly softened as she brought back the richness of that experience. Her body, which had been torqued into a terrified twist, relaxed back to how it had been before she'd signed up for the dreaded audition. I encouraged her to find a physical gesture, what hypnotherapists call an anchoring device, to underline the joyous, soaring feeling while she was experiencing it. She chose the gesture of pressing her thumb to her middle finger, in an "okay" sign to herself.

Harriet practiced the imagery exercise several more times over the next two weeks, both with me and without me, and each time the memory of soaring joy washed over her, she would squeeze her fingers. When it came time for her audition, she was ready. In the moments before singing, she closed her eyes, gestured with her hands, and transported herself back to that feeling. And yes, she sang like an angel.

Conquering anxiety by reentering a fearless mind state, using the directed daydreaming of imagery, is not the same as denying fear or pretending; with imagery, the feeling of courage and optimism is genuinely recaptured.

This principle can be used to advantage to improve attitudes in relationships as well. During an imagery talk I was giving at a women's church group, someone asked me for some pointers for her weary relationship with her husband. She was fed up with him, she said, and couldn't help but stereotype him in her mind, expecting to be bored and annoyed by him. And she was pretty sure he felt the same way about her. Their twelve-year marriage was fairly steeped in ennui. She wanted to interrupt the cycle, but in a low-risk way, with something that wouldn't embarrass or humiliate her—in other words, something he wouldn't even have to notice she was doing.

My suggestion was to see if she could look at her husband freshly, with "beginner's eyes," as the Zen meditators would say, superimposing upon him *the image of him as a potentially interesting stranger.* If she could take a fresh look at him, she might experience a shift in feeling toward him. And, who knows, he might just pick up the change in attitude and reflect it back to her, even amplifying it.

She understood what I was getting at right away, and she nodded and smiled, her face communicating a real openness to the idea. At the end of my talk, she came up to me and expressed an eagerness to go home and give the imagery a try. As I watched the twinkle in her eye and the smile on her face, it was clear to me that she had *already* been doing the imagery and, even before getting home, had begun to experience a change in her feelings toward him. I prayed he wouldn't act like a jerk and discourage this tender, fragile new interest that she had in him.

END-STATE IMAGERY

Another very simple form of imagery is called final-state imagery or end-state imagery. This entails imagining yourself already in the condition or circumstances that you wish for. It is seeing yourself strong, athletic, successful, calm, energized, healthy, admired, cancer-free, loved or loving, forgiving or forgiven. As with feeling-state imagery, you don't need a lot of technical information to do this kind of imagery correctly. You just have to know what you want.

A professional cantor friend of mine frequently uses end-state imagery. He "hears" himself singing a difficult high note that he will need to hit, just a split second before he has to sing it. He claims that when he remembers to do this, he never fails to reach the note, strong and true.

Olympic athletes are trained to use end-state imagery just before their turn at a competition. When we see the diver, poised on the board, in deep concentration, she is rehearsing. She is visually and kinesthetically "diving" in her imagination before she springs off the board. She thus creates in her mind the template of the perfect dive that will guide her real body.

51

A client with arthritis who wanted to use imagery to gain more mobility in her hands and wrists wasn't interested in learning how her joints functioned or what they looked like at the cellular level. End-state imagery suited her just fine. She "saw" and "felt" her wrists moving with greater ease and range, several times a day. Sometimes they were picking things up. At other times they were unscrewing jar tops, typing, opening car doors, or closing safety pins around a grandchild's diapers. She would also "see" her hands less and less swollen and disfigured. All of this qualifies as good end-state imagery.

ENERGETIC IMAGERY

Another all-purpose kind of imagery that doesn't require particular scientific knowledge of cells or organs in the body is what I call energetic imagery. This imagery follows ancient Chinese and Ayurvedic Indian ideas about health. According to these systems of medicine, increasingly accepted in the West, a healthy body has a good, strong current of "life force" (also called *chi*, *prana*, vital energy, electromagnetic energy, and many other things) that *flows freely* through it, moving in a general looping pattern through various energy centers in the body (see the illustration on the next page). It is thought that this snaking pattern is the origin of the concept of Kundalini, the energy that is said to rise like a serpent, up through the body. These energy centers are sometimes called *chakras*, and they channel all the waves and particles that we are ultimately made of. (Keep in mind that when we subject our *particles* to closer scrutiny, we discover that they, too, are just *waves*. It turns out we are nothing but motion, *vibration*, cleverly disguised as solid stuff. Oddly enough, modern theoretical physics and ancient Chinese

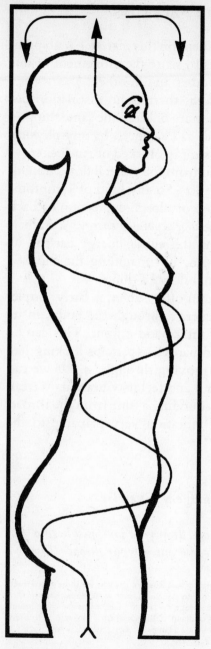

Arrow shows direction of energy flow

Natural flow of energy up through (the *chakra* system of) the body.

Illustration by Katherine Janus Kahn

medicine are in cozy agreement on this matter.) With practice, we can train ourselves to sense the movement of this
energy flow in our own bodies and in others.*

With this idea of health, there is no distinction between mind and body. They are one and the same thing—
energy. Illness of any kind, as evidenced by any physical
or emotional problems, is simply blocked or stuck energy,
chi that has gotten withheld from the general flow, tipping
the body-mind out of balance. So any kind of symptom,
be it coronary artery disease or ulcers, depression or back
spasm, is *some form of blocked or separated energy*. We rebalance our bodies by guiding this subtle energy back to its
free flow in the body again, by imagining the blocked
energy rejoining the normal flow of things.

The imagery this system offers, then, is fairly simple:
sensing the free flow of energy through the body, in its
natural looping curves of intake and output. This can be
seen visually as waves and particles (perhaps looking like
the dots on a TV screen) moving through us. Or we can
hear it as a humming sound and feel its vibration. We can
intensify this imagery by sounding a tone from the throat,
making the sensation of vibration very palpable to the
body.

Toning Imagery Exercise

*Take a deep breath and drop your jaw, just letting
a tone spontaneously come out of your throat. Try*

---

*Emilie Conrad-Da'oud, Barbara Brennan, and Rosalyn Bruyere are three gifted teach-
ers who know how to show people how to do this in their workshops. Each of these
women has her own school, where she trains clinicians to practice this and other healing
skills. Conrad-Da'oud is based in Woodland Hills, California; Bruyere is in Sierra
Madre, California; and Brennan is in East Hampton, Long Island. Many forms of
meditation and yoga develop this skill as well.

not to think about it, but just use whatever pitch feels right. Then feel the sound as it vibrates through your body. If you move the shape of your mouth as you tone, you'll find that the pitch and location of the sound in your body will change. Some tones will seem to travel all the way down your spine. Others will be more in the top of your head, your face, or your chest or belly. Go ahead and test different pitches and see how they feel. Then take a pitch and send it through your body, feeling it travel all the way up the S-loop that the energy naturally traverses, and out the top of your head. Do this several times, always preceded by a good, deep breath. If you're worried about appearing silly, then just make sure that you have privacy.

We can use the breath to accentuate energetic imagery as well. When we breathe in, we can sense the energy collecting inside of us; breathing out disperses it throughout the body.

Another kind of energetic imagery for general wellness has us imagining that we are pulling up energy from the earth, through the soles of our feet (the sole of the foot is yet another *chakra*, one that is particularly good for the intake of energy). If energy principle number one is that good health means free-flowing energy, then principle number two is that you can never have too much of the stuff. And since everything is made up of these vibrating particles (which aren't really particles anyway, but motion), Mother Earth is loaded with them, and they are ours for the taking, in unlimited supply. If you were to spend a few minutes a day, at odd spare moments, imaging that you were pulling up energy from the earth through the soles of your feet with each inhale, and dispersing it up through your body with each exhale, you would be helping to keep yourself feeling energized and balanced. You might in fact notice an immediate improvement in your mood, finding yourself with an increased feeling of emotional resilience; your long-term benefit could be better general health.

The Reverend Rosalyn Bruyere, a well-known, much respected healer and teacher from the Los Angeles area, has a very deliberate, self-regenerating ritual that she uses between her sessions with her clients. She walks outside and takes a few moments to sense herself pulling in energy from her surroundings. She pulls it up from the ground through her feet, but also with her eyes from the beauty of the mountains in the distance, and with her nose from the scent of the flowers surrounding her. In other words, her central image is that of herself "tanking up" on energy via each and every one of her senses, soaking it all in so that she can cleanse and replenish herself for the next client. She says it may look like she's dawdling, but that nothing could be further from the truth.

When we can train our perceptions to sense the subtle movements of this ubiquitous energy, all through and around us, we can tune into it and even guide it. This opens us up to an intimate dialogue with our own bodies, which in and of itself is healing. It's a very grounding, centering activity, as it locates our awareness right smack in the middle of our bodies, always a good, safe place for it to be. Once there, we can be sensitive to what's happening inside of us, and know early when we are beginning to get out of balance, so we can then make the necessary adjustments.

CELLULAR IMAGERY

Probably the most extensively researched kind of imagery is imagery of events in the body at the cellular level. We know, for instance, that when people imagine their natural killer cells surrounding, attacking, and "poisoning" cancer cells, evidence of increased immune activity appears in the bloodstream and saliva. When people imagine their neutrofils (debris ingester cells) slithering through the walls of blood vessels to "swallow," amoeba fashion, undesirable particles in the tissue, blood samples reveal evidence of heightened neutrofil activity. Most amazing is a study by Mark Rider and Jeanne Achterberg that shows that we can use imagery to *differentially* instruct certain immune cells to attack some things and leave others alone, and they will follow suit. Cellular imagery can thus be very specific, taking dead aim at just what needs fixing, leaving the rest alone. In this sense, it is a far more efficient and desirable process than, say, chemotherapy, which indiscriminately destroys diseased and healthy tissue alike. Unfortunately, we don't yet know how to produce imagery as potent as chemotherapy, so until then, we're stuck with our clumsy chemotherapy for at least a little while longer.

If cellular imagery interests you, it isn't hard to learn how the cells work in a general way to maintain wellness. Subsequent chapters describe in some detail how specific systems work at this level.

It is a magical and inspiring thing to see the way the cells work in the body. What happens when we get a splinter, for instance, is nothing short of a miracle. The inflammation around the splinter—heat, redness, swelling, and pain—is caused by the extra blood at the site. The splinter actually sets off a biochemical alarm, increasing the blood flow around it. (Actually, the blood around the site slows down and sticks to the capillary walls, while new blood continues to arrive.) This extra blood brings white blood cells called neutrofils with it. These are speedy, ravenous, efficient little scavengers that pass through the walls of the blood vessels (which have magically become more permeable for just this purpose) and swarm all over the splinter and the bacteria that rode in on it, trying to eat them and kill them off with enzymes. Many neutrofils die in the process, becoming pus. (Perhaps we should all have more respect for pus! It is, after all, simply the remains of these valiant little soldier cells that died protecting our turf.) This is our first line of defense against infection, and it operates around the clock. Our bodies actually produce these feisty little cells at the inconceivable rate of *80 million per minute*. Imagery that focuses on the nonstop protection they provide is one kind of imagery at the cellular level.

The body's workings at this general level are not hard to understand. But if you have some specific health concerns that go beyond the basic aims of this book, you'll need to do some research to understand exactly how you want your cells to behave. This is not a place to get vague or casual, because cellular imagery can really work.*

I remember a man I met at a diabetes support group who came up to me after an imagery talk to share his puzzlement about why his diabetes imagery wasn't working. He said he was a great believer in imagery and had in fact used it for years to successfully lower his blood pressure. But when he tried using it to help control his diabetes, it actually seemed to make matters worse. I asked him

---

*See the September 1993 special issue of *Scientific American* for clear, accurate diagrams and photographs of cellular activity for a variety of health problems, including cancer, HIV, allergy, infection, multiple sclerosis, and rheumatoid arthritis.

what imagery he was using. He said he knew that sugar was bad for him, so in his imagination he was keeping sugar out of his cells.

Alas, this misguided imagery would certainly be consistent with his elevated blood sugar levels. All of us, but diabetics in particular, who have too much sugar in the blood and not enough of it in the cells, need to get sugar *from* the blood *into* the cells, not keep it out of them. With diabetes, hungry cells can't take sugar in, either because the body doesn't make enough insulin to catalyze the process or because the cells can't use it, even though the body makes enough. The result is a lot of corrosive sugar floating around in the blood, wreaking havoc on blood vessels and organs. And meanwhile, the cells are "starving" in the midst of all this plenty, surrounded as they are by unreachable food.

The man needed his cellular imagery to focus on his insulin finding the hungry cells, connecting with them, and thus enabling them to open up and take in sugar in a steady, balanced way.

Although most people think of cellular imagery as visual, it doesn't have to be. Some people "hear" the cellular activity happening, and others "feel" it. Many of the people I work with use touch to accompany their cellular imagery, precisely to make it more kinesthetic and palpable in the body. Someone interested in boosting his immune cell functioning, for instance, might put a hand over the breastbone, where the thymus, a gland that acts as a major dispatch center for white blood cells, is located.

There is no longer much question that this kind of imagery at the cellular level is effective. Most of the research that has been done has been with studies of this kind of imagery. For the biologically minded, it's a very satisfying form of imagery. And while some people complain that it is overly mechanistic and aesthetically lacking, others find the exquisitely orchestrated dance of the cells to be a profoundly moving, soul-nourishing experience.

PHYSIOLOGICAL IMAGERY

Another kind of imagery found to be effective involves the life-size (as opposed to microscopic/cellular) physical processes in the body. This kind of imagery also requires that you know something about the way the body works. Though you don't have to be "anatomically correct" and know precisely what everything looks like, you do need to understand how things work. The basic dynamics of the body's processes must be correct.

For instance, using this kind of imagery for an autoimmune condition like rheumatoid arthritis requires knowing the difference between rheumatoid arthritis and osteoarthritis. Generally speaking, rheumatoid arthritis *erodes* the bone at the joint and swells the soft tissue surrounding it, whereas osteoarthritis *adds* extra material to the bone. With one, corrective imagery envisions, among other things, "filling in" the bone at the eaten-away places, to return it to a more normal shape and size; with the other, corrective imagery "reduces" the excess buildup on the bone.

We need to know the mechanisms that create our headaches, our allergies, and our low-back pain. So, too, with PMS, high blood pressure, and indigestion. (Imagery for some of these complaints is explored in Chapter 5.) And for good, baseline health maintenance, physiological imagery can be used, for instance, to "see" arteries becoming wider, softer, and more flexible. They can be imagined to be so "slippery" on the insides that plaque has trouble sticking to them.

We can imagine our hay fever subsiding by "sensing" airways opening up and inflamed membranes in the nose and throat shrinking back down. We can feel the softening and relaxing of our back muscle in spasm, sensing it loosen, open, and relax back to its normal size. And, to return to our splinter example, we can sense the inflammation at the site subsiding, with the finger returning to normal size, color, feel, and motility.

In other words, physiological imagery involves understanding the basic, physical mechanics of what is needed to return to balance, and implementing it in the imagination. A little research is required, by consulting your physician or perhaps one of those practical and accurate consumer-oriented health encyclopedias that can be found in any bookstore or library. Sometimes this kind of imagery is easier to understand and execute than its cellular counterpart; sometimes it's more complicated than cellular imagery.

METAPHORIC IMAGERY

Probably the most commonplace kind of imagery is metaphoric imagery. Even imagery that starts out concretely as cellular or physiological will often, over time, wind up in your imagination as something metaphorical. The right side of the brain just naturally leans into using symbols and more poetic ways of looking at things. So it's not unusual for scavenger cells like neutrofils to end up becoming sharks, wolves, or Pac-Men. Natural killer cells that explode cancer cells might become heat-seeking missiles, and insulin that catalyzes sugar intake for hungry cells might take the form of a magic key that opens a cold, creaky castle door to let the sunshine in.

Several practitioners in the field—Jeanne Achterberg and Michael Samuels among them—hypothesize that metaphoric imagery is even more powerful than the rigidly "anatomically correct" sort. They theorize that the right brain is just naturally more predisposed toward symbols (you can look at the content of your dreams and realize how true this is). Moreover, psychology has long felt that the indirectness of metaphors, which don't come at us head-on, can cut through the resistance to change that we might have. However much we may want to change, there is always a piece of us that doesn't. When we don't oppose our reluctance directly, we avoid getting locked into a power struggle with it, and so stand a better chance of slipping around it. (Many of us have learned this the hard way from an oppositional two-year-old.)

Metaphor is truly a form of shorthand. It provides a speedy, powerful way for an image to travel through the body-mind, because a tremendous amount of psychic information can ride in on that one image. And, of course, it can have a profound influence, because symbols, by their very nature, affect *body and soul together*. Symbols are the language of the spirit. They go deep.

One metaphoric image that I sometimes draw on never fails to affect me in exactly this instantaneous, powerful way. I use it to lift me out of a weary cynicism that can sometimes overtake me, especially when I'm physically tired but still have a lot of work to do and many clients to see. Oddly enough, the image wasn't even mine to begin with. A nurse friend gave it to me over twenty-five years ago, when she was telling me how touched she was by the painted toenails on the indigent women she saw being wheeled into surgery at the large metropolitan hospital where she worked. She saw these little red flags on their feet as a touching gesture of human courage and hope in the face of fear, illness, and poverty. I remember being moved and surprised by my friend's comment, appreciating her in a new way after hearing her describe this. I forgot the conversation, but, oddly enough, years later, it was her image of those brave little red toes that popped into my mind and revived my flagging spirits one day. Now I evoke the red toes regularly, whenever I need a reminder of the vulnerability and bravery we all possess.

Another advantage of metaphor is that it offers a ready starting place for our own internal imagery to unfold. Consciously introduced metaphoric imagery will readily give way to spontaneous imagery from deep inside the psyche, because it strikes such a compatible chord with deepest parts of the self. So symbols will shift, change, and develop their own stories with remarkable ease, giving us priceless conversations with heretofore unknown parts of ourselves. We can learn what's been hidden from us that we need to know. Often it's something very simple.

One woman, who struggled for years with her own harsh judgments and punitiveness toward herself, used the image of putting her self-criticism on a raft (in a dark, heavy sack) and sending it downstream. But she found that the image kept getting waylaid. The raft quickly got snagged on some rocky shoals. So she sent some playful otters with nothing better to do to free the raft and send it on its way. But once again, the raft got waylaid, this time by a dam built by some beavers. Clearly, the message from a wise and deep part of herself was, "Not so fast, sister! This is not going to be so easy." The raft metaphor made it possible for her to see how hard it would be for her to let go of her old patterns. And she needed to understand this. She could then adjust her expectations and proceed with a healthier respect for her own resistant pace. The raft metaphor helped her out of the potentially debilitating loop of getting caught in *criticizing herself for not being able to stop criticizing herself*!

PSYCHOLOGICAL IMAGERY

Psychological imagery is imagery that shifts our perception of ourselves. It can help us deal with long-standing psychological dilemmas or some temporary emotional turmoil. In reality, it is inseparable from body-focused imagery, because emotions *are* physical occurrences to the body. Hope, anger, love, and despair are *biochemical* events. And psychotherapists are more and more coming to understand that core psychological struggles appear to have *actual locations in the body*. Someone who feels responsible for everyone and everything might indeed have the weight of the world on very tight, aching shoulders; someone whose psyche is spring-loaded for yet another betrayal may indeed be "stabbed in the back" by chronic lower back pain; and a heartache may indeed look and feel exactly like a *heart ache*.

Because the mind isn't really distinct from the body, psychological imagery might look a lot like physiological imagery, or any of the other kinds I've described in this chapter. The imagery of the woman putting her self-criticism in a bag and floating it away on a raft is clearly psychological, though it takes the form of a metaphor.

Another example is the many kinds of imagery to help someone get through intense grief. Often, a core psychological issue for people who are grieving is their fear of the intense pain that grief carries and a belief that they won't be able to stand it. People will often engage in exhausting, frenetic activity, just to try and avoid the pain. But it doesn't help, because it only wears them down and the feelings don't go away anyway. What they need to do is to stop running and start feeling. Imagery can help take them *through* their feelings instead of *around* them.

One of the things I ask people in this situation to do is to focus their attention on finding the achiest place in their bodies, seeking the actual core of the pain, for just a short while. Then I ask them to tell me what it feels like. If they say, "It's like a knife in my heart" or "It's a stone on my chest," I'll encourage them to work with those metaphors. How ripped open is the heart from the knife? What happens when you try to remove it? How heavy is the stone? Can you breathe under it? Usually, the story will take on a life of its own, and a healing dialogue with the pain can begin.

Sometimes people will just report physical sensations, such as pain in the chest (grief usually sits here), frequently accompanied by tightness in the belly (often the location for fear). It usually helps for them to focus on the sensation and *breathe into it*, very gently and carefully, imagining that the breath is softening the outer edges of the feeling, moving slowly into the center of it. And when people put their own hands on the hurting places, the breathing imagery is usually even more effective. Sometimes they can see the pain as pure, dense, trapped *energy* that the breath releases.

This is by no means limited to grief. Any intense emotion—anger, shame, jealousy, and so on—can be worked with in this way. The result is usually the sense that there is more energy available right away.

Sean, a young woman who had recently learned that her husband had a galloping brain tumor and was expected to die in a matter of weeks, was frantically racing about, driven and panicky, *doing* things: visiting the intensive-care unit, researching her husband's disease, caring for her preschoolers, and working fifty hours a week at her very demanding job. Her brain was spinning, she was losing weight, she couldn't sleep, and worst of all, she was feeling scared, isolated, and disconnected from herself and everyone around her. And, of course, beneath all of that, she was unspeakably sad.

When I asked her what her body felt like, she said, "Like a corkscrew. I feel like I'm all twisted around and I can't straighten out. And the more I talk, the faster I twist." I suggested she stop talking and just breathe into the twist. I put one of my hands over the top of her breastbone, the other at her back, and breathed with her. She "unwound" immediately, at first releasing into heavy sobs and then finally weeping softly. The imagery, augmented by touch, reconnected her back into herself, and even though she then had to contact her sadness, she felt better for it. We almost always feel better when we get back in touch with ourselves, even when what's going on in there is hard. It's the isolation and disconnectedness that kills us.

Sometimes psychological imagery can be interactive. We can use it to conjure up just about anyone. The mellow right side of the brain doesn't nitpick and won't distinguish between "here and there," "now and then," or "alive and dead," to name just a few of the polarities that it finds irrelevant. People in the midst of conflict can get perspective and sometimes even resolution by imagining a dialogue or scenario with their adversary. These imaginary interactions are surprisingly real and can generate major shifts in our perceptions and attitudes.

My pacifist friend Wil, the Pepto-Bismol imager with

HIV infection, developed some imagery to help him get beyond a relationship problem he was having at work. It seems that he was uncharacteristically embattled with a coworker, feeling a lot of anger and resentment toward her. The feeling was mutual and was getting stronger every day. So he invented his own end-state imagery, where he saw himself alone on a stage, receiving thunderous applause from all of his colleagues. Included in the audience was his nemesis, enthusiastically clapping and cheering for him as he happily took his bows. Next he saw *her* up on the stage and himself in the audience, applauding with gusto. (This part was difficult for him to imagine at first, but he stayed with it. It got easier, especially because *she* was being so nice *first*.) He played with this imagery once a day for many weeks.

The imagery got richer. They began to exchange eye contact, from stage to audience, hesitantly at first and more definitively as time went on. This evolved into some stronger personal acknowledgment, in the form of nods and smiles between them. By the time the imagery had progressed to their presenting each other with bouquets, followed by warm, heartfelt embraces, their real-life relationship had begun to thaw in earnest. They were close, committed friends when Wil died five years later.

Imagery can be used to generate empathy and compassion for someone else. One woman, a social worker at a staff in-service training session, used imagery to get some insight into her behavior toward her overweight adult daughter, who lived at home with her. She was worried about her and, though she tried to motivate her to lose weight, was ineffective at it. She was frustrated and angry. In an imagery exercise, she *became* her daughter, entering her daughter's body, and then looked over at herself, the mother, through her daughter's eyes. She was startled by her reaction. What she experienced was a sinking feeling in the pit of her stomach as she looked over at her "mother," feeling an overwhelming sense of weariness and despair, a profoundly sad certainty that she would not be able to measure up to her expectations.

At the close of this exercise, she expressed great sorrow and regret for what she'd been doing to her daughter. She'd "gotten it" at a very gut level. The imagery interrupted a fruitless power struggle between mother and daughter that was doomed to yield no winners.

SPIRITUAL IMAGERY

Some people would say that *any* kind of imagery is spiritual imagery—that even imagining going to a favorite place, feeling attuned to its beauty, and filling up with a deep gratitude just to be there once more is a kind of spiritual imagery. Many people, as I mentioned earlier, feel a profound kind of awe at the exquisitely orchestrated, microscopic dance of the cells, protecting and renewing the body with such finely honed intelligence. And the experience of tuning into the sensation of "energy" is a spiritual one; indeed, if energy is the stuff of all things in the universe, then feeling it inside of us connects us to everything in the world. This sense of oneness with all things is the essence of mystical contact with the Divine. So, too, opening ourselves up to the spontaneous unfolding of an intuitive metaphor that carries with it wisdom from the deepest part of ourselves is what some people would say is hearing the voice of God.

Nonetheless, some imagery has content that deliberately tries to access spirit per se, and this is what I'm calling spiritual imagery. It is imagery that aims directly for connection with God, or for an opening into a larger world that extends beyond our concrete everyday reality. It might be a world of angels and spirits; or it might be a world where everything in it—the grass, the clouds, and even the air—is vitally alive and dancing with sparkling, divine energy.

When I was getting feedback from several chemotherapy patients at University Hospitals about the imagery I was developing for them, the image most frequently cited as the favorite surprised me. It was an image tucked away on the second side of the audiotape, the last of a series of affirmations that said, "I know that I am held in the hands of God, and I am perfectly, utterly safe." I had included this sentence somewhat gingerly and hesitantly, knowing that some people would be put off by its overtly religious-sounding sentiments. And a few people were. But so many more were grateful for it that I kept it there. To this day, the letters I get from people mention this one sentence more than any other as the words that provide the most comfort and meaning for them.

If we were to look at our most popular prayers and scriptural passages, we would find that they all contain rich, metaphoric imagery that resounds deeply inside us and stays with us. For instance, "The Lord is my shepherd, I shall not want. He leadeth me beside the still waters . . ." is vivid, evocative imagery, filled with powerful messages of comfort and safety. Perhaps all good prayer is a form of imagery; perhaps all good imagery is a form of prayer.

One friend of mine, David, is a gifted psychologist, successful, practical, and grounded, who looks a lot like a football player, which he once was. David believes he has an angel at his back at all times. His angel, he tells me, is a huge fellow, about seven feet tall, with a wingspan about as wide. David doesn't always see him. Sometimes he just *feels* him, as a kind of warm presence at his back.

Now, regardless of whether this is a bona fide angel or just an image of an angel, David's traveling buddy provides him with a sense of continuing support, companionship, and safety. And because of this, I know that his angel actually does in fact protect him from stress and maintains his body's health and well-being. Needless to say, David doesn't tell everyone about his humongous sidekick, but in his heart, he knows he's there.

Many people experience the presence of a loved one who has died. Sometimes they hear the person's voice, giving some pithy, characteristic advice, or they might feel him close by, or even see him, plain as day. At first my clients will talk about these things with great hesitancy, afraid I'll think them deluded by grief and longing, or else just plain crazy. Actually, from what I can tell, the experience of these "visitations" is more the norm than not. I encourage people to acknowledge and work with these "images," invoking them, conversing with them, or asking them to go away if that's what they'd prefer. From what I've been able to tell, most of these "visitors" are pretty cooperative and will do what is asked of them.

People can also use imagery to converse with themselves as children, lost loved ones, an abstract wisdom figure, their own inner guidance, or their idea of God. Certainly, looking to religious images for inspiration and support isn't exactly a revolutionary idea. People invoke the familiar images from their religious upbringing, Jesus or Mother Mary, favorite saints or hosts of angels, Buddha or Allah, the Shechinah or the Holy Spirit. Some might simply see themselves surrounded by unknown but beautiful and loving beings. Whatever nourishes the soul, opens the heart, and lifts the spirit is good for our health. Whatever awakens us to the larger perspective and allows us to glimpse a sweeter, more loving reality, either inside or outside of us, is imagery that serves us well.

```

         ┌─────────┬────────┐
         │         │        │
         │         │        │
         │         │        │
         │         │        │
         │  CHAPTER 3        │
         └─────────┴────────┘
```

CHAPTER 3

IMAGERY EXERCISES
FOR YOUR
GENERAL HEALTH

This chapter offers you a wide sampling of different kinds of imagery. One is no better than the other, but you will probably find yourself naturally preferring some over others. I'll be presenting them to you by the categories that I laid out and described in Chapter 2.

One caution: Try not to make quick assumptions about what will suit you and what won't. Sometimes the imagery that is the most "foreign" is what works best, precisely because we *don't* have any preexisting experience with it. This leaves the freewheeling right brain open to do what it loves to do best: create, invent, and imagine.

You may want to record some of these "scripts" in your own voice or have someone read them to you. If you do, make sure the words and phrasing suit you, with long enough pauses between images to give your imagination the time it needs. (There is a tendency, especially at first, to read a little too fast.) Perhaps you'll just want to read the whole sequence or a segment to yourself first and then silently imagine the scenario for a few moments after. Experiment and see what feels best.

If you do read the imagery aloud, the ellipses (. . .) indicate a brief pause. Spaces between paragraphs encourage longer pauses. And (pause) suggests an even longer one. Again, you be the judge of the pacing and do what feels right for you.

Although you can work with imagery anywhere, it's a good idea to try to find a comfortable, quiet area in your house or office (or even your car) where you know you won't be disturbed. If you can shut off the phone and avoid other kinds of disruption, go ahead and do so. And if you use the same location each time, you'll create an instant association between that spot and a readiness to get down to work (very much like what we tell our kids about doing their homework).

Play background music if you think it will help you relax. It does for most people, and it offers the added advantage of covering sounds that could distract or annoy you. (If you find that some environmental sounds are unavoidable, try to incorporate them into your actual imagery.)

You may want to try out different kinds of music to see what suits you. Some kinds of New Age music lend themselves very well to relaxation; so does a lot of classical music, particularly movements identified as "adagio" and "largo." (Several suggestions for musical pieces are offered on page 37.) You can also get tapes that have simple sounds from nature—the ocean, rain on a roof, a waterfall, or birds in a meadow. Ideally, the volume should be loud enough that you don't have to strain to hear it, but soft enough that it doesn't compete with the imagery.

Soft lighting also helps, unless you have a problem falling asleep too easily, in which case, brighter lights are preferable. So, too, sitting up is better than lying down, if staying awake is a challenge. And half-closed eyes are preferable to eyes that are completely shut, if you're quick to fall asleep. Otherwise, adopt whatever position you need to make yourself comfortable and relaxed.

Whether you are sitting up or lying down, it's good to have your head, neck, and spine straight. That way, you don't get a major kink in your neck after being still for such a relatively long time.

Many people experience a noticeable change in body temperature after imaging in the altered state. If you find that you're someone who gets colder, make sure you have a sweater or blanket with you; if you're one of those who get warmer, also dress accordingly. There's no point in being uncomfortable.

And remember to be kind and respectful toward yourself. Don't try to force the experience on yourself if you're not in the mood. You can't anyway—coaxing might work, but forcing will defeat your purpose. If you're only up for five minutes' worth of imagery, five good minutes is better than fifteen distracted, resentful ones. And always feel free to adjust and edit the imagery anytime it doesn't feel quite right.

It's usually good to have the same beginning cues to start your imagery. Deep, deliberate, full breathing is a good device, because it's an internal body experience that's available at all times, and it immediately relaxes.* Just as with the consistent use of the same location and music, in a very short time a powerful association is made. The

---

*The exception is with asthmatics and others who have trouble breathing comfortably.

body-mind experiences the place, the music, and the breathing, and right away goes into a rich, deep, altered state. After a short while, you won't need all these cues. But it's a good way to begin.

I usually have people settle comfortably into their chairs (or beds, the couch, or the floor if they're lying down) and feel the support of whatever is under them. Then I generally ask them to take at least two or three deep breaths, exhaling fully each time. This slows people down and readies them for deeper work. And of course, the lovely thing about using the breath as a cue is that it is right under our noses all the time. Perhaps you can't always have your regular spot or your music with you, but your breath will always be right there.

FEELING-STATE IMAGERY

Feeling state is imagery that alters your mood. Although it is simple imagery, it is powerful and effective. This first exercise is simple, all-purpose imagery that takes you to a favorite place for a brief but effective "vacation." It's good for shifting a stressed mood to one of peace and calm. One suggestion: If you're someone who could spend hours deciding which place is the absolutely *best* place to go to, see if you can choose one acceptable place ahead of time, just for the sake of this exercise, and try to stick with it. (My experience from workshops is that about one in eight people can be so relentlessly exacting and perfectionistic with themselves that they could spend the entire time of the exercise searching for the most relaxing place, which gets them very frustrated and upset.)

Favorite Place Imagery
(approximately 8 minutes)

To begin with, see if you can* position yourself as comfortably as you can, shifting your weight so that you're allowing your body to be fully supported. by your chair or couch or whatever is supporting you. Try to arrange it so that your head, neck, and spine are straight.

And taking a deep, full, cleansing breath . . . inhaling as fully as you can . . . breathing deep into the belly if you can . . . and breathing all the way out . . .

And again . . . breathing in . . . and this time, seeing if you can send the warm energy of the breath to any part of your body that's tense or sore or tight . . . and releasing the tension with the exhale . . . and breathing it out . . .

So you can feel your breath going to all the tight, tense places, loosening and warming and softening them . . . and then gathering up all the tension and breathing it out . . . so that more and more, you can feel safe and comfortable, relaxed and easy, watching the cleansing action of the breath . . . with friendly but detached awareness . . .

And any unwelcome thoughts that come to mind, those too can be sent out with the breath . . . released

---

*Feedback at workshops has taught me to keep the language in these narratives *suggesting* as opposed to *commanding*. Most people will more easily respond to the words "see if you can position yourself" than to the more imperative "position yourself." I also recommend using the verb form known as the present participle (e.g., "taking" rather than "take") as a way of avoiding commands. Many people balk at being told what to do in the imperative voice, even if that voice is their own!

with the exhale . . . so that for just a moment, the mind is empty . . . for just a split second, it is free and clear space, and you are blessed with stillness . . .

And any emotions that are rocking around in there . . . those, too, can be noted, and acknowledged, and sent out with the breath . . . so your emotional self can be still and quiet . . . like a lake with no ripples . . .

And now, imagining a place where you feel safe and peaceful and easy . . . a place either make-believe or real . . . a place from your past . . . or somewhere you've always wanted to go . . . it doesn't matter . . . just so it's a place that feels good and safe and peaceful to you . . .

And allowing the place to become real to you . . . looking around you . . . taking the place in with your eyes . . . enjoying the colors . . . the scenery . . . looking over to your right . . . and over to your left . . .

And listening to the sounds of the place . . . whatever they might be . . . wind or water . . . birds or crickets or a whole multilayered texture of sounds . . . just so your ears can become familiar with all the beautiful music that your special, safe place offers up to you . . .

And feeling whatever you're sitting against or lying upon . . . or perhaps feeling the texture of the ground beneath your feet . . . whether it's sand or pine needles or grass . . . or you might be in a cozy armchair . . . or sitting on a nice, warm rock in the sun . . .

And feeling the air on your skin . . . crisp and dry . . . or balmy and wet . . . perhaps you are inside, feeling the warmth of a cozy fire on your face and hands . . . or maybe you are outdoors, and there's just the subtlest caress of a fragrant, gentle breeze . . . so just enjoying the feel of the place on your skin . . .

And smelling its rich fragrance . . . whether it's the soft, full scent of flowers . . . or sharp, salt sea air . . . sweet meadow grass . . . or maybe the pungent smell of peat moss in the forest . . .

So just taking it all in, all the richness of it . . . with all of your senses . . . becoming more and more attuned to your safe and beautiful special place . . . just feeling thankful and happy to be there . . .

And letting your body soak in the vibrance of the place . . . letting its richness penetrate all the way into you . . .

So just letting the beauty of the place nourish you . . . taking it with every full, deep breath . . . all the way down into your belly . . . all the way down to the tips of your toes . . . feeling the penetrating warmth and power of the place . . . soaking into your skin . . . down through muscle and bone . . . all the way to each and every cell . . . reaching down to the peaceful stillness at your very center . . .

(longer pause)

And so . . . knowing that you can call forth this place . . . whenever you wish . . . once again, feeling yourself sitting in your chair or lying down . . . just breathing in and out, very rhythmically and easily . . . and very gently and with soft eyes, letting yourself come back into the room whenever you are ready . . . knowing in a deep place that you are better for this . . .

And so you are . . .

This next exercise also provides all-purpose imagery that shifts your mood. I call it Imagery to Reinhabit the Body, because that's what it does: It gets us out of our heads (or, worse yet, the stratosphere) and moves us back down into our bodies. People experience this imagery as a very settling, grounding experience. It slows them down. It clears out their heads. Their pulse rates get slower and their voices become softer and lower. Their inner center of gravity gets closer to the ground, a much safer (and less tippable) place for it to be.

It's an especially good antidote for times when you feel scattered and fragmented, or when your head is just too cluttered. Try it on a day when you've expended so much energy on the people and things outside of yourself that you've lost touch with your center.

Imagery to Reinhabit the Body
(approximately 10 minutes)

See if you can position yourself as comfortably as you can, shifting your weight so that you're allowing your body to be fully supported. Try to arrange it so your head, neck, and spine are straight.

And taking a deep, full, cleansing breath . . . exhaling as fully as you can . . . (pause) . . . and another . . . deep into the belly . . . pause . . . and again, breathing out as completely as you can . . .

And gently allowing yourself to turn your attention inward . . . focusing inside for just this next while . . . to see how your body feels . . . to take a gentle, curious inventory of your insides . . . just a friendly interest in what's happening in there . . .

Interested in your own well-being . . . looking to see how you are for just this moment . . . what your energy level is like just now . . . noticing your mood . . . still breathing deeply and easily . . . and looking inward with the honest, neutral eye of a camera . . .

And feeling where your body might be tight or tense or sore . . . and where it feels loose and open . . . so just letting your awareness move around the insides of your body . . .

Starting perhaps with your head . . . checking to see how it feels inside your head . . . whether it feels tight and congested . . . or comfortable and open . . . (pause) . . .

And moving down into your neck and shoulders . . . curious about any tightness or heaviness there . . . (pause) . . .

And down into your chest . . . continuing to breathe smoothly and deeply . . . sensing how it feels around your heart . . . (pause) . . . aware of any sensation there . . . heavy or tight . . . or spacious and open . . . (pause) . . .

Moving around into the length of the back . . . noticing how your back feels all along the spine

. . . (pause) . . . all the way to your tailbone . . .
(pause) . . .

And coming back around . . . to see how it feels
inside your belly . . . continuing to breathe deeply
and easily . . . feeling what is happening all through
your abdomen . . . noticing in a friendly but detached
way any tension or fear that might be held there . . .
(pause) . . .

And moving your awareness down into your bottom . . . seeing how it feels along your whole pelvic
floor . . .

And down into your legs . . . feeling any tightness
or rigidity in the legs . . . all the way down to the
feet . . . all the way to the tips of the toes . . .

So just doing this gentle, curious inventory of the
inside of your body . . . noting where it might feel
denser, heavier . . . and where it feels looser, lighter
and freer . . .

And taking a couple more deep, full breaths . . .
all the way down into the uncomfortable places . . .
breathing the warm energy of the breath into the
heart of the discomfort . . . and breathing it out . . .

And again, sending the breath into the core of the
tightness . . . letting it warm and loosen and soften
all around and through it . . . and then breathing
the discomfort out, deeply and fully . . .

So just taking this space to reacquaint yourself
with this body of yours . . . your steadiest companion
. . . your oldest friend . . . and listening to it . . .
and acknowledging it . . .

And letting your awareness sink down into it . . . allowing your spirit to settle all the way down into your body . . . softly and easily rolling into every corner . . . like a gentle, misty fog . . .

And just letting yourself feel the fullness of it . . . breathing fully and easily into every corner of your being . . . softly acknowledging the sore, weary places . . . and the strong, solid places . . . no praise, no blame . . . just noting what is so . . . and remembering how good it feels to connect back into yourself . . .

And so, whenever you are ready . . . taking another full, deep breath . . . and gently, with soft eyes, coming back into the room whenever you are ready . . . knowing in a deep place that you are better for this . . .

And so you are . . .

END-STATE IMAGERY

End-state imagery lets us see ourselves the way we wish to be. This next imagery exercise allows you to imagine yourself in a peak performance state, doing what you love to do, without a thought and in perfect harmony with yourself. It's open-ended enough to allow you to fill in the particulars of your own circumstances and activities.

This imagery can be used to rehearse or improve an already fine performance or to help you learn an altogether new skill. It can also give you what you need to just *begin* your performance, if you're one of those beleaguered folks who labor under the curse of performance jitters and/or chronic procrastination (as many gifted people do). It is also a kind of feeling-state imagery, in that it will lift your spirits and so be good for your health.

Again, if it looks like you are going to have trouble choosing an activity to focus on, try to pick one in advance, arbitrarily choosing anything, for the sake of the exercise. It may, in fact, be a good idea to start out with an activity that you're not terribly invested in or concerned about, just to get the hang of it at first. If you're a blocked, frustrated writer, you might want to start out using this exercise for your tennis game. Then, once your imagination has you playing championship tennis, you might be ready to move on to applying it to your writing.

Peak Performance Imagery
(approximately 8 minutes)

To begin with, see if you can position yourself as comfortably as you can, shifting your weight so that you're allowing your body to be fully supported. Try to arrange it so that your head, neck, and spine are straight.

And taking a deep, cleansing breath . . . inhaling as fully as you comfortably can . . . (pause) . . . and exhaling fully . . . (pause) . . .

And again . . . breathing deep into the belly if you can . . . (pause) . . . and breathing out, as completely as possible . . . (pause) . . .

And once more . . . breathing in and sending the warm energy of the breath to any part of your body that's tense or sore or tight . . . and releasing the tension with the exhale . . . so you can feel your breath going to all the tight, tense places, loosening and softening them . . . and then gathering up all the tension and breathing it out . . . so that more and more, you can feel safe and comfortable, relaxed and easy, watching the cleansing action of the breath . . . with friendly but detached awareness . . .

And any unwelcome thoughts that come to mind, those, too, can be sent out with the breath . . . released with the exhale . . . so that for just a moment, the mind is empty . . . for just a split second, it is free and clear space, and you are blessed with stillness . . .

And any emotions that are rocking around in there . . . those, too, are noted, and acknowledged, and sent out with the breath . . . so that your emotional self can be still and quiet, like a lake with no ripples . . .

And now, imagining yourself doing something . . . whatever activity you've chosen to work with for now . . . (pause) . . .

And seeing yourself engaged in that activity . . . in all your surroundings . . . noting where you are . . . looking around you . . . taking in the sights . . . the sounds . . . the smells . . . there may even be tastes . . . so just letting yourself become aware of your environment with all of your senses . . . even the feel of your clothes on your body . . . and the air on your skin . . .

And noticing the way your body feels to you . . . in whatever way that it's positioned . . . (pause)

. . . or moving . . . with friendly but detached awareness . . .

And now, if you would, see if you can imagine what it feels like to be utterly absorbed in this activity . . . fully and completely . . . so focused and involved in it that you've lost all sense of yourself . . . moving beyond a sense of time and place . . . just doing what you do . . . freely and easily . . . flowing in perfect sync with yourself . . . the dancer becoming the dance . . . the singer becoming the song . . . (pause) . . .

So just enjoying the perfect harmony of mind and body merging into the doing and being . . . feeling the grace of being so crisply focused . . . and yet so soft and steady . . .

Enjoying elegant intelligence of the body . . . knowing what to do without being told . . . effortless . . . graceful and easy . . . merging in perfect pitch with its music . . . suspended in time and space . . . like a beautiful bird, aloft on the back of the wind . . .

Holding this moment . . . breathing it in . . . kissed by perfection and the joy of being alive . . . and filled with gratitude for just being . . .

And so whenever you are ready . . . taking another deep, full breath . . . (pause) . . . and exhaling fully . . . (pause) . . . knowing you can come back to this place, and the richness of this experience, whenever you wish . . .

And so . . . breathing rhythmically and easily . . . whenever you are ready . . . allowing yourself

*to come back into the room whenever you are ready
. . . knowing in a deep place that you are better for
this . . .*

And so you are . . .

ENERGETIC IMAGERY

Energetic imagery makes use of the idea that plentiful,
free-flowing electromagnetic energy *(chi)* is the stuff a
healthy person is made of. This is all-purpose wellness
imagery and, in that sense, similar to the imagery that
precedes it.

Although you're welcome to sit down for this imagery, you may find that standing or walking is more compatible with it. The second exercise makes use of the
contact of your feet with the ground, so lying down
doesn't make as much sense as it usually might. But as
always, feel free to experiment and discover what suits
you best.

Energy Moving Imagery
(approximately 8 minutes)

*You may want to start by shaking your body out
a little. Then see if you can find a comfortable way
to sit or stand. You may want to gently sway back
and forth a little with your eyes closed to try to get
a sense of where your center of gravity is.*

*And now, letting your eyes relax, and taking a
nice full breath . . . (pause) . . . and breathing out
as completely as you can . . . (pause) . . .*

*And again . . . taking in a slow, even, full breath
. . . (pause) . . . and exhaling as fully as you comfortably can . . . (pause) . . .*

*And still again . . . this time imagining that you
are inhaling a magical supply of healing energy with
the in-breath . . . perhaps seeing it in sparkling microdots of color . . . or colors . . . or maybe hearing
a subtle hum as it dances into your body . . . or
perhaps just feeling on the inside the subtle energy
moving into you . . .*

*And with the exhale, sensing this energy dispers-
ing all through your body . . . moving into every
corner . . . all the way to the tips of your fingers and
the very ends of your toes . . . just feeling this subtle,
tingling magic traveling all through your body . . .*

And again . . . breathing it in . . . (pause) . . .

*And then releasing it all through your body with
the exhale . . . feeling more and more the delicate,
dancing presence of this energy . . . as it moves
through your body . . .*

*And again . . . breathing it in . . . and as you
exhale, feeling it as it moves toward anyplace that
might be a little denser or darker or heavier . . .
drawn toward anyplace that might feel blocked . . .
or uncomfortable . . . or tight . . . and sensing it
gently surrounding those places . . . softening them
. . . loosening them . . . massaging and opening
them . . .*

*And feeling the heavier places beginning to shift
and move . . . like a logjam beginning to break free
. . . slowly at first . . . but then faster and easier*

. . . as each new breath helps to move it along . . .
gently and easily . . . neither pushing nor pulling
. . . just a gentle invitation to float along free . . .

And again . . . taking the energy in with the
inhale . . . and this time, making a sound with the
out breath . . . loud or soft, high or low . . . whatever wants to come out . . . whatever feels right . . .
and letting the tone fill your body . . . vibrating and
humming all through you . . . as you feel the energy
of it . . . softening and releasing any pockets of painful feelings stored in the body . . . beginning to
feel the achy, sore, weary places start to shift and
move . . .

And again . . . breathing in deeply and fully . . .
(pause) . . .

And opening your throat and toning again . . .
maybe this time a little louder or softer . . . or maybe
higher or lower . . . whatever feels right to you . . .
and feeling the vibration all through your body . . .
and feeling the sound releasing your energy . . .

And one more time . . . taking a rich, full, deep
breath . . . (pause) . . .

And dropping your jaw . . . opening your throat
. . . And letting whatever tone that wants to, come
out with the exhale . . . rich and deep and strong
. . . or soft and subtle and high . . . whatever feels
right . . . and feeling the vibration move through
your body . . . healing, soothing, and energizing
you . . . from head to toe . . .

So simple but so powerful . . . like recharging a
battery . . . able to feel the difference on the inside

. . . subtle but resilient and strong . . . and so, with your own soft, open attention . . . continuing to focus your awareness on the sensations of energy, moving inside your body now . . . and perhaps remembering how good it feels to connect with yourself . . .

Thankful to have such a simple device available to recharge and renew your body and spirit . . . whenever you wish . . . and knowing in a deep place that you are better for this . . .

And so you are . . .

The next energetic imagery exercise is done while walking. It's good for people who respond strongly to a visual sense of their environment. It also works well for people who have trouble sitting still.★

It is designed to help you "tank up" on energy from your surroundings. The net effect is extraordinarily peaceful and grounding and at the same time uplifting and energizing. Beautiful surroundings help, but even they aren't absolutely necessary.

One suggestion, though: While you are engaged in this imagery, *try not to relate to anyone* who passes you on your walk. In order to derive maximum benefit from the exercise, it's best if you can avoid expending *any* energy on anyone else, even with something as simple as eye contact, a smile, or an innocent "hello." The idea is to *just take energy in*—through all your senses—and put nothing out. We rarely do this, and sometimes we need to. You'll

---

★These are two indicators of the likelihood of being a classic "Type A" personality. This group is apparently more prone to heart disease, diabetes, and stroke than the general population. This segment of the population corresponds very closely to the category Deepak Chopra calls Pitta in the ingenious Ayurvedic medicine framework described in his book *Perfect Health*.

BELLERUTH NAPARSTEK

be surprised when you find how much energy you've been dissipating on what might be fairly meaningless social contact.*

It may well be that, especially with this exercise, you'll start out using a tape of this script, but will then dispense with it, preferring to do your walking accompanied only by nature and unimpeded by any other sounds.

Walking Imagery Exercise
(for as long as you feel like walking)

To begin with, shake your body out a little. Then see if you can find a comfortable way to stand, dropping your shoulders, unlocking your knees, and turning your attention to the inside of your body. See if you can sense where you feel your center of gravity to be, and try balancing that center comfortably between your feet.

And just take a nice full, cleansing breath . . . (pause) . . . and breathe it out as fully and completely as you can . . . (pause) . . .

And again . . . a slow, even, full breath . . . (pause) . . . and exhaling as fully as you comfortably can . . . (pause) . . .

And now, beginning to walk at an easy, thoughtful pace . . . fully conscious of your surroundings . . . opening all of your senses to your environment

---

*I'm not suggesting that friendly smiles and nods to strangers on the street are always a waste of time. Sometimes it feels absolutely wonderful, and besides, civilization needs this kind of social glue to maintain itself. But sometimes we need to unplug our external scanners and just retreat inward.

. . . enjoying the colors . . . whatever subtle arrangements of form, light, and shadow . . . (pause) . . . all the richness of the sights and sounds that surround you . . . (pause) . . . letting your ears become more and more attuned to the variety of sounds, some obvious and others muted . . . just taking it all in . . .

And letting your skin feel the presence of your surroundings . . . letting the air caress you and enter your pores . . . as you smell all the fragrances carried to you . . . each separate scent . . . as you continue to walk at an easy, steady pace . . .

Each step solidly connecting with the ground . . . and even enjoying that . . . the feel of your feet on the ground . . . the support of the earth beneath them . . . so letting your awareness linger there awhile . . . at the place where your feet make contact with the earth . . .

And noticing the increasing acuteness of your perceptions as you go along . . . how the colors around you might seem to become more and more vivid and defined . . . how even the sound of your feet on the ground seems louder, crisper . . . more distinct . . . how your senses flourish from all this mindful attention . . .

Perhaps even becoming aware of the tastes in the air . . . sometimes the air can have a taste . . . or just feeling the motion of the body . . . the steady roll of your hips in their sockets . . . the tingle of energy in your hands as you move along . . .

So just receiving the whole world through your senses . . . feeling an expansion in your chest as you breathe the richness of your surroundings into your heart . . . fully present . . . soft and rich and full . . .

And again turning your attention to the feel of the ground beneath your feet . . . feeling the whole earth supporting you . . . and perhaps even sensing the vibrating hum of the planet beneath you . . . alive and generous . . . breathing its own powerful breath into your feet . . . and feeling the energy of the earth move into you . . . filling and nourishing you with every step . . . rich and boundless . . .

Every step a gift . . . every breath . . . every sight and sound savored with gratitude . . . feeling yourself enveloped by riches . . . soaking in the joy of being alive . . . fully present to the moment . . . shoulders and heart open . . . moving with balance and strength, steady and centered . . .

Feeling full and supple and strong . . . aware of energy in infinite supply . . . yours to take in whenever you wish . . . requiring only your own mindfulness . . . only that . . . and the whole world is yours . . .

And so, feeling peaceful and easy, continuing for as long as you wish . . . ending whenever you are ready . . . knowing in a deep place that you are better for this . . .

And so you are . . .

(Continue your walk for as long as you wish, either replaying this segment or perhaps with just the sounds of your surroundings.)

CELLULAR IMAGERY

There are many kinds of cellular imagery that I could offer you in this section. But the obvious choice for cellular imagery is immune system imagery. The activity of the immune system in monitoring and protecting our health is a cellular-level operation on many fronts. The dance of all the different kinds of immune cells in the body is a dazzling tour de force by a multitalented corps de ballet, so well trained and so exquisitely choreographed, they take the breath away.

The imagery that follows is designed to encourage the steady and strong defense of the body, but with discrimination and balance, so that the body isn't turning against itself.* This imagery can be done by people with autoimmune disease (where the immune system is too aggressive and attacks the body's own tissue), because it emphasizes a *discriminating* defense of the body, which knows how and when to quit.

One caution: I do not recommend this imagery for HIV-infected people. Because of the way the HIV cycles through the body, HIV imagery requires some very particular and crucial variations.†

This imagery guides you to place one hand over your thymus (just below your collarbone, under the breastbone) and the other over the belly, where the Peyers Patches are tucked away in the lining of the intestinal walls,

---

*This is what happens with autoimmune diseases, such as rheumatoid arthritis, multiple sclerosis, lupus, ALS, myasthenia gravis, Krohn's disease, and a host of other conditions.

†The virus lies dormant in the nucleus of the T cell and becomes activated when the T cell goes to work, doing its job for the immune system. So with HIV, you want to encourage any T cells harboring the inactive HIV to *go to sleep and stay asleep*. Other T cells can pick up the slack and take up active patrol. (Remember, cells can be differentially directed with imagery to behave in very specific ways.) The *Health Journeys* tape for HIV has complete, specialized imagery for this situation.

to encourage your kinesthetic awareness of the imagery and to remind those immune-related glands that they are expected to cooperate with this imagery. This placement of your hands becomes what is called in hypnotherapy an anchoring device. After a certain amount of routine practice with this imagery, you will be able to put your hands on these two spots, anytime and anywhere, and immediately and automatically experience the responses that your body had to this imagery. Thus you can sit in a boring meeting and, with a subtle gesture, covertly boost your body's immune function!

Immune Cell Imagery
(approximately 14 minutes)

Please start by making yourself comfortable, shifting your weight so you can feel fully supported, whether you are sitting or lying down. Try to see to it that your head, neck, and spine are straight . . . letting your eyes softly close if that is comfortable for you . . .

And taking a deep, cleansing breath . . . inhaling as fully as you comfortably can . . . (pause) . . . and breathing out . . . (pause) . . .

And again . . . taking the breath deep into the belly if you can . . . (pause) . . . and breathing out, as fully as possible . . . (pause) . . .

And once more, breathing in and imagining that you're sending the warm energy of the breath to any part of your body that's sore or tense or tight . . .

and releasing the tension with the exhale . . . so you can feel your breath going to all the tight, tense places, loosening and softening them . . . and then, gathering up all the tension and breathing it out . . . so that more and more you can feel safe and comfortable, relaxed and easy . . . watching the cleansing action of the breath . . . with friendly but detached awareness . . .

And any unwelcome thoughts that come to mind, those, too, can be sent out with the breath . . . released with the exhale . . . so that for just a moment, the mind is empty . . . for just a split second, it is free and clear space . . . and you are blessed with stillness . . .

And any emotions that are rocking around in there . . . those, too, are noted, and acknowledged and sent out with the breath . . . so your emotional self can be still and quiet, like a lake with no ripples . . .

And now, putting the flat palm of one hand over your breastbone . . . a little below the base of your neck . . . and your other hand on the center of your belly . . . also flat palm down . . .

And sensing that a soft, healing warmth is coming out of your hands . . . and softly entering your body . . . gently penetrating into skin and muscle and bone . . . layer by layer . . . surrounding and soaking into the glands that house your immune cells . . . stimulating and revitalizing them . . . the two-lobed thymus beneath your breastbone . . . and the little clusters of Peyers Patches in the belly . . . and perhaps even feeling a ripple of fresh appreciation for

*the constant support and protection they provide . . .
gratitude for keeping you safe and strong and
well . . .*

*And sensing the two lobes of the thymus plumping
up, warm and pink and full . . . like a peach, ripen-
ing in the warmth of the sun . . . and so, too, with
the tiny clusters of the Peyers Patches . . . soaking
in strength and purpose . . . tight, full, strong little
sacs, bursting with vitality . . .*

*Feeling the thymus, somewhere beneath your
hand, gearing up to send forth whatever armies of
defending cells that are needed . . . to anyplace in
the body . . . to eliminate anything that might harm
you . . . loyal and ready . . . thousands of miraculous little soldier cells, highly trained, focused, and
intelligent . . . utterly committed to your well-being
. . . knowing what to attack and what to leave
alone . . .*

*Sensing the movement of these remarkable, trust-
worthy little soldier cells . . . highly trained, discriminating, and intelligent . . . moving out from
their dispatch centers . . . all through your body . . .
combing tissue and fluid for anything that might
contribute to your discomfort . . . bypassing the
healthy cells . . . respecting your own territory . . .
and seeking out the cells occupied by the virus invad-
ers, which impose uninvited on the warm generosity
of your body . . .*

*And knowing that your crack corps of highly
trained fighter cells can immediately see where an
uninvited virus has made itself a home . . . by the*

telltale markings that the virus leaves on the cell . . . like muddy footprints at the entrance of a house . . .

So sensing the patrolling T cells, sighting the marked cells . . . quickly surrounding them . . . and destroying them with a deft thrust . . . like a foil in the hands of a master fencer . . . deftly perforating the membrane of the cell . . . and shutting it down forever . . . (pause)

And knowing that these miraculous little T cells can even clone themselves if necessary . . . knowing they can spread out in multiples of themselves and scurry after other infected cells that try to proliferate . . . ferociously pursuing each and every infected cell . . . with commitment, focus, and determination . . .

So just sensing the movement of these loyal defenders . . . dispatched from the powerful gland under your breastbone . . . and moving all through your body . . . protective and loyal . . . (pause)

And aided by other special troops . . . helper cells that survey the action and call in more troops as needed . . . and suppressor cells that are able to see when the last of the enemy is gone, and thus call the fighting to a halt . . . calming down any overzealous fighter cells with no enemy left to attack . . . sending them home . . . with the sense of a job well done . . . satisfied and calm . . .

And sensing, too, all the varieties of other elite troops that protect the body . . . marshaled from their many locations . . . with specialties of their own . . . some especially trained to identify chaotic, mu-

*tant cancer cells that will occasionally start to form
. . . knowing to quickly surround them . . . and
penetrate and poison them . . . deftly and easily . . .
before they can begin to make trouble in any way
. . . so just taking a moment or two to sense the
movement of these intelligent, intensely focused cells
. . . spring-loaded to mobilize themselves at the mer-
est beginnings of a threat . . . (pause)*

*And sensing the brilliant transformation of other
cells . . . cells designed to fight bacteria . . . cells
that wait in the spleen and lymph nodes, like bored
recruits, until they are needed . . . and then, exquisitely changing form . . . producing charged, perfectly programmed little missiles . . . sent through
the blood, straight to their target . . . brilliant, versatile
cells that also know how to magically clone themselves
. . . so they can overpower large numbers of infiltrators
. . . however many there might be . . . and so restore
the body's integrity and strength . . .*

*And sensing, too, the cleanup crew of feeding cells
. . . the loyal, sturdy foot soldiers, who cart the
debris off the battlefield . . . leaving the tissue fresh
and clean and new . . . quickly coming in to clean up
whatever broken bits have been left behind . . . leaving
fresh, clean space for healthy new cells to grow . . .*

*So just feeling gratitude for this exquisitely orches-
trated system of protection . . . for all this activity
on your behalf . . . all through your body . . . all
day and night . . . a vigilant, effective, nonstop
patrol . . . a noble and brave army of dedicated soldiers, utterly committed to your well-being . . . intelligent and discriminating . . . only attacking where*

necessary . . . and knowing when to leave well enough alone . . .

So just breathing in wonder and gratitude for this everyday miracle . . . happening inside your own body . . . every moment of every day . . . no less miraculous for its constancy . . . and breathing out . . . (pause) . . .

And again, breathing in this sense of safety and protection . . . (pause) . . . and breathing out . . . fully and easily . . . (pause) . . .

And so . . . feeling peaceful and easy . . . very gently and with soft eyes . . . coming back into the room whenever you are ready . . . knowing you are better for this . . .

And so you are . . .

PHYSIOLOGICAL IMAGERY

Just as the obvious choice for cellular imagery is the immune system, a "natural" for physiological imagery is the cardiovascular system. The imagery I offer you here is designed to even out your blood pressure and help you maintain a strong heart and healthy, open arteries. With the new research findings from groundbreaking internist Dean Ornish at the Preventive Medicine Research Institute at the University of California, San Francisco, we now know that coronary artery disease can, in fact, sometimes be reversible without surgery. So some of the images here are of reversing the beginnings of coronary artery disease. For good measure, I've included some imagery about metabolizing blood sugar, to increase digestive efficiency.

This can be helpful whether you're diabetic, prediabetic, or just plain normal.

Cardiovascular Imagery
(approximately 9 minutes)

Please try to position yourself as comfortably as you can, shifting your weight so that you're allowing your body to feel fully supported. See if you can arrange it so your head, neck, and spine are straight.

And just taking a deep, full, cleansing breath . . . inhaling as fully as you comfortably can . . . (pause) . . . and exhaling fully . . . (pause) . . .

And again . . . breathing deep into the belly if you can . . . (pause) . . . and breathing out, as fully as possible . . . (pause) . . .

And once more . . . breathing in and sending the warm energy of the breath to any part of your body that's tense or sore or tight . . . and releasing the tension with the exhale . . . so you can feel your breath going to all the tight, tense places, loosening and softening them . . . and then gathering up all the tension and breathing it out . . . so that more and more, you can feel safe and comfortable, relaxed and easy, watching the cleansing action of the breath . . . with friendly but detached awareness . . .

And any unwelcome thoughts that come to mind . . . those, too, can be sent out with the breath . . . released with the exhale . . . so that for just a mo-

ment, the mind is empty . . . for just a split second, it is free and clear space, and you are blessed with stillness . . .

And any emotions that are rocking around in there . . . those, too, are noted and acknowledged, and sent out with the breath . . . so that your emotional self can be still and quiet, like a lake with no ripples . . .

And now, gently allowing yourself to turn your attention inward . . . focusing inside for just this next while . . . to see how your body feels . . . and turning your attention, if you would, to the subtle sensation of your blood, moving through your body . . . perhaps feeling its steady warmth, moving all through you . . . perhaps hearing it vibrate and hum as it moves along . . . or maybe seeing the exquisite, intricate pattern of veins and arteries . . . wide and powerful at your center . . . and delicate and filigreed at your outermost edges . . . so just taking a few moments to acknowledge your remarkable system of circulation . . . so strong and steady . . . (pause) . . .

And aware that the blood moving through your body, so steadily and easily, seems to have an exquisite intelligence of its own . . . a built-in ability to repair and heal everything it touches . . . and you can feel it, softly and easily rolling along . . . gently expanding the vessels as it goes . . . making more room for the rich supplies that it brings . . .

And softening the walls of the arteries as it moves along . . . making them into more flexible, enduring *stuff . . . keeping the inner lining slick and smooth and shiny . . . with no place for debris to cling to it . . .*

And strengthening and replenishing the arteries' weaker spots . . . should there be any . . . and perhaps there are none . . . but in case there are . . . shoring up any thin places along the walls . . . as the rich, steady supply continues to roll along . . . like a gentle river . . . rich and full and nourishing . . . bringing everything that's needed to fortify the walls . . . safely and easily . . . as constant and steady as the earth rolling through the heavens . . .

And sensing how the steady flow gradually reduces whatever small collection of unwanted debris might have begun to gather, here and there along the sides . . . gently and safely eroding whatever tiny buildup that might have accumulated in the lining . . . perhaps some small, fatty streaks . . . or possibly a few older, more crusty places . . . gradually and safely eroding them . . . wearing them down to smooth, clean slickness . . . safely expanding each vessel, big or small . . . the wide, powerful ones around the heart . . . in the neck and shoulders and thighs . . . and the smaller ones that make up the whole, miraculous network . . . down to the tiniest, laciest filigree of capillaries in the fingers and toes . . .

Opening the narrower places . . . and allowing for an even, steady flow . . . gentle and strong in the wide, smooth, soft arteries . . .

And dissolving any matter in the bloodstream itself . . . turning any beginnings of clotting into tiny microdots . . . and dispersing them, safely and easily . . .

A gentle, steady river, feeding the hungry tissue along its banks . . . and just sensing how the sugar and nutrients in the blood leach out into the surrounding field of tissue . . . soaked up by the hungry cells . . . in a steady, continuous supply . . .

And feeling the hungry tissue respond . . . sensing the cells plump up to full strength from this steady, generous source . . . as new life and energy return . . . organ and muscle and bone rebuilding . . . as cells replace themselves . . . and the body charges up with strength and purpose . . . remembering its power and vitality . . .

And so . . . feeling all through your body the penetrating warmth and power of this awareness . . . grateful for your capacity for healing and renewal . . . strong and steady and resilient . . .

And so, once again . . . feeling yourself in your surroundings . . . taking a deep, full breath . . . gently and with soft eyes . . . coming back into the room whenever you are ready . . . knowing you are better for this . . .

And so you are . . .

METAPHORIC IMAGERY

For metaphoric imagery, I've chosen some all-purpose imagery that can apply to your health or to anything else about yourself that you want to change. Remember, you don't have to *understand* metaphoric imagery logically in order for it to work; you can just keep playing with it and developing it in its symbolic or abstract form. I realize that for those of you who are more cognitively oriented, it probably makes no sense whatever that you could change something without a full, clear, logical grasp of the process, but believe me, you can. Give it a try. See if you can put your analyzing self on hold for a while to experience what can happen—the potential benefits, especially for "left-brainers," are bountiful.

This first metaphoric imagery exercise is located *in the body* for maximum sensory immediacy and kinesthetic impact. The second gives you *perspective and distance* from an issue, by using a screen as the vehicle that removes you from yourself. A screen or a stage can be a powerful vehicle for getting around your own resistance to change, whether it be overt or even hidden to you. You may find that each exercise suits you for working with very different kinds of issues. Experiment and see.

And you might want to keep a pad of paper and a pen next to you, to jot down some notes when you are done with each exercise. Interesting further developments can sometimes happen while you're writing.

With both exercises, remember that you can repeat them and pick up where you left off; or you can repeat them and just deepen the impact of the same imagery each time you use it. For some people, there is a subtle but cumulative effect over time; for others, the impact is immediate and dramatic with the very first try.

Again, some of you will do best by choosing the issue ahead of time; it may change or stay the same as you experience the imagery. Others will prefer not to con-

sciously choose an issue, but instead see what the unconscious mind decides to come up with.

Transforming an Issue Located in the Body
(approximately 11 minutes)

*See if you can position yourself as comfortably as
you can, shifting your weight so that you're allowing
your body to be fully supported. Try to arrange it so
your head, neck, and spine are straight.*

*And taking a deep, full, cleansing breath . . .
exhaling as fully as you can . . . (pause) . . . and
another . . . deep into the belly . . . (pause) . . .
and again, breathing out fully and comfortably . . .
(pause) . . .*

*And gently allowing yourself to turn your atten-
tion inward . . . letting come up into your awareness
a physical or emotional issue that you'd like to transform . . . just taking whatever time is needed . . .
(pause) . . .*

*Clearing away a space in your mind . . . so that
something that needs changing can appear . . . some
issue . . . or way of being . . . perhaps a physical
problem . . . or an attitude of yours that you've
grown weary of . . . whatever wants to present itself . . .*

(longer pause)

*And letting yourself be curious to see where this
issue sits in the body . . . where it is felt . . . so*

taking a moment to let the body show you where this is held . . . (pause) . . . and acknowledging its presence, with neither praise nor blame . . . just a neutral, honest nod of recognition to it . . . and letting yourself feel its presence . . . noticing where it perhaps has always been . . . or where it has moved to now . . .

So just letting it appear to you in any form it wants to . . . allowing it to be there, as you sense its nature . . . becoming more and more clear and defined as you focus your attention on it . . . whether it seems hard or soft . . . slippery or spongy . . . dense and heavy, or light and airy . . . if it feels like there are edges to it . . . and how much space it occupies . . . checking it out with the neutral eye of a camera . . . neither denying it nor exaggerating it . . . but just seeing what is there . . . not with your mind, but with your senses . . .

And checking to see if it has a color . . . or colors . . . (pause) . . . and if it has any sound or sounds that you can hear . . . a hum or a whine . . . a rumble or a roar . . . any special pitch or rhythm . . .

Perhaps there is even a smell or a taste to it . . . so just checking to see if maybe there is an aroma associated with it . . . or a familiar taste in your mouth . . .

Letting yourself experience this issue . . . with all of your senses . . . in a state of friendly but detached awareness . . . watching it . . . feeling it . . . neither pushing it away nor pulling it close . . . but just letting it be . . . observing it freshly, with genuine curiosity . . .

(longer pause)

And now . . . watching as it starts to shift and change . . . very naturally and of its own accord . . . if it wants to . . . and maybe it doesn't . . . and if it doesn't, that's all right, too . . . that's a good thing to know, if it doesn't . . . but if it does . . . and it might . . . allowing it to begin to transform in whatever direction it's inclined to go . . . letting it happen in its own way . . . in its own time . . .

Just allowing it to begin to shift . . . whether this means a change in color . . . or density . . . size or temperature . . . sound or smell . . . whether it's something expanding or shrinking . . . softening or hardening . . . whatever wants to happen . . . whatever doesn't want to happen . . . it needn't make sense to you . . . and it needn't go to completion . . .

And feeling the shift in your body . . . however subtle and delicate . . . or bold and dramatic it may be . . . just letting yourself feel the change on the inside . . . as something starts to transform . . . still feeling detached but curious . . . friendly and interested . . .

So just letting yourself watch the shift . . . noticing whatever happens . . .

(longer pause)

And whenever you are ready . . . giving yourself permission to put this away for now . . . knowing you can bring it back and visit this again whenever you wish to . . . knowing it will keep . . . that this is fine for now . . .

And so setting this aside for now . . . with appreciation for whatever it may be about . . . however clear or vague . . . giving it the respect it deserves . . . for all its stubborn complexity . . . and giving yourself respect and appreciation as well . . . understanding that even lack of clarity and unfinished business can be illuminating . . .

And so . . . taking a deep, full breath . . . deep into the belly, if you can . . . (pause) . . . and breathing all the way out . . . fully and completely . . . (pause) . . .

And again . . . another soft, full breath . . . all the way down to the bottom of the belly . . . (pause) . . . and all the way out . . .

Gently and with soft eyes . . . turning your attention back into the room whenever you are ready . . . knowing in a deep place that you are better for this . . .

And so you are . . .

The second metaphoric exercise uses the device of a screen to provide distance and perspective from an issue, and to help you get around whatever resistance to changing it you might have. Although the language is my own, it's derived from an imagery exercise that I learned years ago from Kenneth Pelletier, an important innovator in the field who has influenced many current practitioners.

Again, you don't "spell out" your issue cognitively, but instead let it appear to you in symbolic form. This form may or may not make sense to you. In fact, you may start out deliberately picking one symbol and find that, midexercise, something else upstages it, taking over the screen. If that happens, it means that your unconscious is really running the show. You can trust it to do a wise and responsible job, even if its spontaneous promptings initially make no sense to you.

So start this exercise with some idea of the issue you want to work on and how you want it symbolized. For instance, you might decide that your resentment of your husband's family is the issue you want to work on, and your symbol of it is a huge, immovable rock. You might stay with the rock for the whole exercise; or you might find that the rock has become red-hot lava, and later you realize that you're really angry at your husband for being a wimp with your in-laws. If you have trouble choosing a symbol, go to something more concrete, using actual images of people and things, and see how that works. There are only three ground rules here. First, try to keep the issue something about *you* and therefore something that's in your power to change. Second, don't try to work the issue cognitively during the exercise. If you feel you must analyze the meaning of the symbols, that's fine—just do it later. In fact, if you jot down notes immediately afterward, they will help you with your analysis. But if you repeat the exercise to take the imagery further, go back to the symbolic images, letting them do whatever it is they do or don't do, without analysis. And, finally, don't get discouraged. Sooner or later, this imagery really takes off.

A client of mine who had been working for a long time to get beyond her long-standing, debilitating fury at her father had a powerful experience with this imagery, what she tearfully referred to as a minor miracle. The image that came up for her on the screen was of red-hot coals. That was what her anger at her father felt like to her. As the imagery progressed, the coals spontaneously started to change, getting hotter and hotter, the way coals do, ultimately turning a grayish white. Even though she wasn't supposed to be "thinking," she nonetheless was anticipating that the coals would evolve into ashes and blow away. Then, from out of nowhere, a long-forgotten scene from her childhood popped onto the screen. It was her preadolescent self and her dad, quietly toasting marshmallows over the white-hot charcoal of a campfire, feeling very close and companionable. The original sweetness of that relationship, before the complications of puberty and family tragedy changed it, washed over her. She reexperienced the closeness and the nourishment that they once had between them, forgotten in all the pain that had followed. She came away from that imagery feeling like a different person, and all the anger that she'd been trying so hard to cast off floated away.

Transforming a Symbolic Issue on a Screen
(approximately 12 minutes)

To begin with, see if you can position yourself as comfortably as you can, shifting your weight so that you're allowing your body to be fully supported . . . and your head, neck, and spine are straight . . .

And taking a couple of deep, cleansing breaths . . . inhaling as fully as you comfortably can . . . (pause) . . . breathing deep into the belly if you can . . . and breathing all the way out . . . (pause) . . .

And again . . . breathing in . . . seeing if you can send the warm energy of the breath to any part of your body that's tense or sore or tight . . . (pause)

. . . and releasing the tension with the exhale . . . (pause) . . .

So you can feel your breath going to all the tight, tense places, loosening and warming and softening them . . . and then, gathering up all the tension and breathing it out . . . so that more and more you can feel safe and comfortable, relaxed and easy, watching the cleansing action of the breath . . . with friendly but detached awareness . . .

And any unwelcome thoughts that come to mind . . . those, too, can be sent out with the breath . . . released with the exhale . . . so that for just a moment, the mind is empty . . . for just a split second, it is free and clear space, and you are blessed with stillness . . .

And any emotions that are rocking around in there . . . those, too, are noted and acknowledged, and sent out with the breath . . . so your emotional self is still and quiet . . . like a lake with no ripples . . .

And now, imagining a place where you feel safe and peaceful and easy . . . a place either make-believe or real . . . a place from your past . . . or somewhere you've always wanted to go . . . it doesn't matter . . . just so it's a place that feels good and safe and peaceful to you . . .

And allowing the place to become real to you . . . looking around you . . . taking the place in with your eyes . . . enjoying the colors . . . the scenery . . . seeing each and every detail . . . looking over to your right . . . and over to your left . . .

And listening to the sounds of the place . . . what-ever they might be . . . wind or water . . . birds or crickets . . . or a whole blend of sounds . . . just so your ears can enjoy the unique music of this special place . . .

And feeling whatever you're sitting against or lying upon . . . or perhaps feeling the quality of the ground beneath your feet . . . whether it's sand or pine needles or grass . . . or you might be in a cozy armchair . . . or sitting on a nice, warm rock in the sun . . .

And feeling the air on your skin . . . either crisp and dry . . . or balmy and wet . . . or perhaps you are inside and can feel the warmth of a cozy fire on your face and hands . . . or maybe you are outdoors, and there's just the subtlest caress of a fragrant, gentle breeze . . . so just enjoying the feel of the place on your skin . . .

And smelling its rich fragrance . . . whether it's the soft, full scent of flowers . . . or the sharpness of salt sea air . . . sweet meadow grass . . . or the pungent smell of peat moss from the forest floor . . .

And as you become more and more attuned to the safety and beauty of this place . . . feeling thankful and happy to be there . . . you might notice a kind of tingling . . . a pleasant, energizing something in the air all around you . . . something that contains expectancy and excitement . . . a sense that some-thing wonderful is just about to happen . . .

And as you look out in front of you . . . just a few feet in front of you . . . you begin to discern that there is a kind of transparent screen forming there

. . . *getting more and more opaque and solid as you look at it . . .*

And as you watch the screen, with a kind of peaceful curiosity, you gradually become aware that a form is beginning to appear on it . . . becoming more and more defined as you watch . . . until the three-dimensional image of a symbol is quite clear . . . and you can see that this is the symbol of whatever it is that you want to work with or change in a positive direction . . . becoming more and more defined and crisp and clear . . . and you might be aware that you can watch it with a kind of alert but peaceful detachment . . . calm and curious . . . and you may even want to have it turn, slowly and steadily, so you can see it from every angle . . . (pause) . . .

And noting anything about this symbol on the screen . . . whatever colors it might have . . . any sounds associated with it . . . any vibration or hum . . . or perhaps even a kind of music . . .

There might be a fragrance or smell to it . . . or it might have a quality of hardness or softness . . . it could be heavy or light . . . big or small . . . bitter or sweet or sour . . . so just taking these next few moments to let yourself be curious . . . observing whatever is on the screen in a state of friendly, detached interest . . . very carefully . . . and with all of your senses . . .

(pause for 15–20 seconds)

And now, if you would, see if this image on the screen is willing to shift or change in any way . . . see if it will move in any direction it wants to go

. . . *without pushing it or pulling it . . . but just letting it transform, if it wants to . . . and if it doesn't, that's all right, too . . . in fact, it's good to know, if it doesn't want to . . . but if it does . . . and it might . . . just watching the shift occur . . . in a state of calm and curious detachment . . . observing this transformation, however subtle or bold . . . with all of your senses . . .*

Understanding that it need not be complete . . . it need not make any sense to you . . . but just seeing the shift . . . with all of your senses . . . for however long it takes . . . calm and curious . . .

(pause for 15–20 seconds)

And now . . . understanding that you can come back and work further with the screen and your images whenever you wish . . . letting it take however long it needs to take . . . and knowing perfectly well that whatever amount of time it takes will be exactly the right amount of time . . . you can begin to let the image fade . . . and again, seeing the screen . . . and letting that fade, too . . .

And once again, seeing your special surroundings . . . feeling safe and comfortable, relaxed and easy . . . although perhaps the colors are brighter . . . perhaps the sounds are more vivid . . .

Breathing deeply into your belly . . . allowing yourself to come back into the room whenever you are ready . . . knowing in a deep place that something powerful has happened . . . that you are better for this . . .

And so you are . . .

PSYCHOLOGICAL IMAGERY

For psychological imagery, I've chosen one exercise that relates to you internally, to your own feelings, and one that's about a relationship that you have with someone else. The first is for releasing grief—either the intense kind that all of us have when we lose someone or something we deeply love, or the everyday, garden-variety losses and disappointments that pile up on us from day to day, as we live our lives. Either kind can give us "grief" in many other, and often more physical, ways.

Most of us aren't aware of carrying around grief, like so much excess baggage on our hearts. Yet, when we meditate or get very quiet, sometimes the first thing that comes up in us is a kind of sweet sadness. Our eyes fill and our noses start to run, as this sensation moves through us. Yet it feels okay. And indeed, what could be bad about it? We are releasing our top layer of grief and lightening our hearts.

Both of these exercises begin with the mood-altering Favorite Place Imagery that appears alone at the beginning of this chapter. This is to set the tone and encourage a strong reverie state for the intense imagery that follows.

The grief imagery has a strong spiritual component as well, along with many other elements designed to convey a powerful sense of support. The essence of the psychological message is that although important people, places, and times may have left us, our loving feelings for them are ours to keep forever. In psychotherapy jargon, these feelings become our "transitional object," the "blankie" we can cart around with us like an unsteady toddler, until (and if) we are ready to let go of it.

*Imagery to Release Grief**
(approximately 14 minutes)

Please get comfortable . . . shifting your weight so that you're allowing your body to be fully supported . . . with your head, neck, and spine straight . . .

And taking a couple of deep, full, cleansing breaths . . . inhaling as fully as you comfortably can . . . sending the warm energy of your breath to any part of your body that is sore or tense or tight . . . and releasing the discomfort with the exhale . . . so that you can feel your breath going to all the tight, tense places . . . loosening and softening them . . . and then, gathering up all the tension . . . and breathing it out . . . so that more and more you can feel safe and comfortable, relaxed and easy, watching the cleansing action of the breath . . . with friendly but detached awareness . . .

And any distracting thoughts or feelings that you might have . . . those, too, are sent out with the breath . . . so that inside you can be still and quiet, like a lake with no ripples . . .

And now, imagining a place where you feel safe and peaceful and easy . . . a place either real or imaginary . . . a place from your past . . . or somewhere that you've always wanted to go . . . it doesn't matter . . . just so that it's a place that feels good and safe and peaceful to you . . .

*This guided meditation is essentially taken from the *Health Journeys* series, *For People Experiencing Grief*, by Belleruth Naparstek, produced by Time Warner AudioBooks, Los Angeles, California, 1993.

116

And allowing the place to become more real to you . . . looking around you . . . taking the place in with your eyes . . . enjoying the colors . . . the scenery . . . looking over to your right . . . and over to your left . . .

And listening to the sounds of the place . . . whatever they might be . . . wind or water . . . birds or crickets . . . just so your ears can become familiar with the music of your special place . . .

And feeling whatever you are sitting against or lying upon . . . or perhaps feeling the quality of the ground beneath your feet . . . whether it's sand or grass . . . a pine-needle forest floor . . . or you might be in a cozy armchair . . . or sitting on a nice, warm rock in the sun . . .

And feeling the air on your skin . . . either brisk and breezy . . . or soft and still . . . crisp and dry . . . or balmy and wet . . . perhaps you are inside, feeling the warmth of a cozy fire on your face and hands . . . or maybe you are outdoors, and there's just the subtlest caress of a fragrant, gentle breeze . . . so just enjoying the feel of the place on your skin . . .

And smelling its rich fragrance . . . whether it's the soft, full scent of flowers . . . or the pungent smell of salt sea air . . . or sweet meadow grass . . . or maybe the pungent smell of peat moss in the forest . . .

And as you become more and more attuned to the safety and beauty of this place . . . feeling thankful and happy to be there . . . you begin to feel a kind of a tingling on your skin . . . a pleasant, energizing something in the air all around you . . . something that contains expectancy and excitement . . . and you know with some certainty . . . that it is good and right to be here . . . that there is magic in this place . . . and something wonderful is just about to happen . . .

And as that certainty settles around you, you notice that the tingling is taking on a kind of a glow . . . that the air is alive . . .

And from somewhere above you, a cone of powerful white light is softly and steadily moving down, forming a tent of vibrant, tingling energy all around you . . . surrounding and protecting you . . . illuminating everything it touches with exquisite brightness . . . highlit definition . . . vibrating color . . . giving everything it shines on a fresh, new beauty . . .

You can feel the air around you intensifying . . . glowing . . . dancing with sparkling energy . . . and with a sense of gentle wonder for such stunning beauty, you feel the light moving down into your body . . . softly entering your head and neck . . . moving into your shoulders and torso . . . sending a warm, vibrating softness all through your body, all the way down into your legs and feet . . . moving with deliberate intelligence to the deepest places where pain and fear are stored . . . and feeling the spaces begin to soften and open . . . as you breathe into them . . . fully and deeply . . .

You suddenly realize you are not alone . . . that you are aware of a warm presence all around you

. . . and looking around, surprised but not surprised . . . you see that you are surrounded by gentle, loving beings . . . immediately recognizable as allies . . . smiling and nodding in the remarkable light . . . warming you with their protective presence . . .

One of them softly approaches you . . . and with a wonderful, deep, gentle look, directly into your eyes . . . gently touches the center of your chest . . . with warmth and softness . . . sending comfort and solace deep into your heart . . . waves of nourishing, loving comfort, right into the heaviness of your heart . . . soothing the torn, jagged places . . . opening and warming and softening all around the pain . . .

And you can breathe deeply, filling your whole body with this generous, healing energy . . . perhaps letting the tears begin to melt the armor around the heart . . . as the eyes that gently see you, nod and smile . . . showing you that it is understood, how much hurting you have done . . . it is understood, the stony-cold aloneness you have felt . . . the wordless ache of longing . . . the stinging regret . . . the disappointment of interrupted dreams . . . all the pain is understood . . . breathtakingly intense at one moment . . . and heavy and dull the next . . . all of it is understood . . .

You feel the warmth of this awareness begin to collect and radiate through your entire chest . . . sending compassion and forgiveness and reassurance to every corner of your being . . . soft and easy . . . sweet and rich and full . . . as you breathe into the opening spaces of your heart . . . widened by the warmth of the healing hand . . .

And suddenly you are certain . . . you know with your whole heart . . . with your whole being . . . that there is a place where nothing is lost . . . where all the love and sweetness, direct or disguised, that you have ever felt is still alive . . . that all the love you have ever felt for anyone at any time is alive and well in the vast spaces of your own open heart . . . placed there forever . . . rich and nourishing and boundless . . . always available to sustain you . . .

Breathing in to touch it . . . breathing out to let it move through you . . . feeling the body soften . . . sending a gentle, healing forgiveness all through you . . . a new compassion for yourself . . . a different way of looking . . .

Perhaps you understand that you are being shown . . . that even this terrible pain can be a teacher . . . showing you something you need to know . . . about yourself . . . about who you are . . . and who you are becoming . . .

You know that even this will look different to you in time . . . when you know more about who you have become . . . when you are connected to your life in a new way . . . and the pain has permanently softened . . . when this has become part of the depth and richness of the texture of your life . . .

In the deep, gentle warmth of the eyes that look at you, you see that it is understood that you have seen this . . . that you have had a glimmer of your own healing . . . that you understand that nothing has been lost to the vastness of the heart . . . that the whole world spins there . . . and so you can begin to return to the peaceful stillness at your center . . . breathing in to touch it . . . breathing out to let it move through you . . .

And as your gentle band of allies smiles and nods . . . your special one says, "Remember, we are always here. It is you who come and go. Call for us anytime and we will come."

And gathering up a handful of the glowing, vibrating light, places it in your heart for safekeeping . . . your own special supply . . . to use as needed . . .

And so, feeling peaceful and easy . . . you watch as the light slowly begins to withdraw . . . returning to wherever it came from . . . until it is gone altogether . . . for now . . . knowing it is yours to call forth again, whenever you wish . . .

And taking a deep, full breath . . . feeling the widened spaces that are now opened . . . you once again see yourself in your safe and peaceful surroundings . . . feeling safe and easy . . . although perhaps the colors around you are brighter . . . the air more alive . . .

You might feel that something powerful has happened . . . that a major shift has occurred . . . and will continue to occur . . . with or without your conscious working on it . . .

And you can see very clearly that you can call forth this place . . . the powerful healing cone of light . . . the special ones . . . whenever you wish to further the work that you have already done . . .

*And so . . . feeling yourself sitting in your chair
or lying down . . . breathing in and out, very rhythmically and easily . . . gently and with soft eyes . . .
coming back into the room whenever you are ready
. . . knowing in a deep place that you have done
important healing work . . . that you are better for
this . . . and so you are . . .*

This next exercise is designed to elicit genuine empathy and give you new insights into another person. Once
you get a feel for it, you may want to use it for fresh
perspective into relationships that are deadlocked, boring,
or downright difficult; or to reconnect with a very special
person from your past. It's very versatile, and works
equally well for family, friends, and colleagues. It's a
practical tool for daily living. But it also gives us a glimmer of the amazing beings that we really are. We get an
inkling of the enormous reach of our intuitive capacity
with this imagery. And mind you, this is just the tip of
the iceberg!

For openers, choose someone with whom you really
want to improve your end of the relationship. It doesn't
matter if the person is living or dead. And, as always, don't
be surprised if you consciously choose one person, and
midway through the exercise, he or she switches to someone else. If this happens, try to go along with it and see
what happens.

The screen in this imagery provides the distance and
perspective to make it easier for your psyche to go along
with the imagery. You may want to write about your
experience after this exercise, so keep a notebook and pen
handy. This can help integrate and further develop whatever occurs.

Imagery to Increase Empathy for Another*
(approximately 10 minutes)

See if you can position yourself as comfortably as you can . . . shifting your weight so you're allowing your body to be fully supported . . . head, neck, and spine straight . . .

And taking a couple of deep, full, cleansing breaths . . . inhaling as fully as you comfortably can . . . sending the warm energy of your breath to any part of your body that's tense or sore or tight . . . and releasing the discomfort with the exhale . . . so that you can feel your breath going to all the tight, tense places . . . loosening and softening them . . . and then gathering up all the tension and breathing it out . . . so that more and more, you can feel safe and comfortable, relaxed and easy . . . watching the cleansing action of the breath . . . with friendly but detached awareness . . .

And any distracting thoughts or feelings you might have . . . those, too, are sent out with the breath . . . so that inside, you can be still and quiet . . . like a lake with no ripples . . .

And now . . . imagining a place . . . where you feel safe and peaceful and easy . . . a place either make-believe or real . . . a place from your past . . . or somewhere you've always wanted to go . . . it doesn't matter . . . just so it's a place that feels good and safe and peaceful to you . . .

---

*Essentially taken from the *Health Journeys* series *For People Working on Their Relationship*, by Belleruth Naparstek, produced by Time Warner AudioBooks, Los Angeles, California, 1993.

And allowing the place to become real to you, in all of its dimensions . . . looking around you . . . taking the place in with your eyes . . . enjoying the colors . . . the scenery . . . fully appreciating every detail with your eyes . . . looking over to your right . . . and over to your left . . .

And listening to the sounds of the place . . . the motion of wind or water . . . the music of birds or crickets . . . or a whole blend of sounds . . .

And feeling whatever you are sitting against or lying upon . . . or perhaps feeling the quality of the ground beneath your feet . . . whether it's sand or pine needles or grass . . . or you might be in a cozy armchair . . . or sitting on a nice, warm rock in the sun . . .

And feeling the air on your skin . . . either crisp and dry . . . or balmy and wet . . . perhaps you are inside, feeling the warmth of a cozy fire on your face and hands . . . or maybe you are outdoors, and there's just the subtlest caress of a fragrant, gentle breeze . . . so just enjoying the feel of the place on your skin . . .

And smelling its rich fragrance . . . whether it's the soft, full scent of flowers . . . or sharp, salt sea air . . . sweet meadow grass . . . or maybe the pungent smell of peat moss in the woods . . .

And as you become more and more attuned to the safety and beauty of this place . . . feeling thankful and happy to be there . . . you might begin to feel a kind of tingling . . . a pleasant, energizing something in the air all around you . . . something that contains expectancy and excitement . . . a sense that something wonderful is just about to happen . . .

And as you look out in front of you . . . just a few feet before you . . . you begin to discern that there is a kind of transparent screen there . . . getting more and more opaque and solid as you look at it . . .

And as you watch the screen with a kind of peaceful curiosity . . . you gradually become aware of a human form beginning to appear on it . . . becoming more and more defined . . . until the three-dimensional image of a person is quite clear . . . someone you want to understand better . . . or resolve something with . . . appearing on the screen . . . in whatever characteristic posture they have . . . wearing whatever it is that they wear . . . doing whatever it is that they do . . . crisp and clear in every dimension . . .

And surprised but not surprised, you see that you can softly and easily enter the screen . . . to have a closer look . . . undetected by them, you can slip into the screen . . . and have a slow, detached, curious walk around them . . . seeing them from every angle . . . the profile . . . and the back . . . and the other side . . .

And experiencing the feel of the air around them . . . the sounds of the breathing or the voice . . . the smells that surround them . . . just slowly moving around them . . . experiencing a full, rich awareness of them . . . with all of your senses . . .

And now . . . in the safe, magical space of the screen . . . for the sake of your own learning . . .

somehow, for just a short while . . . sliding past the boundaries and slipping into the body of this other person . . . entering this other awareness . . . and breathing their breath . . . for just a brief while . . .

And if there is any resistance to doing this, just gently noting it, and allowing yourself to soften all around it . . . for the sake of understanding more . . . to learn what you need to know . . . just an experiment . . . feeling what it is like to be in their body . . . breathing their breath . . . looking down and seeing the hands and the feet . . . the clothing . . .

And feeling what is happening in the heart . . . (pause) . . . the belly . . . (pause) . . . the muscles of the back and the neck . . . (pause) . . . open and curious as to how it is in there . . .

And seeing out from their eyes . . . what the world looks like . . . sounds like . . . feels like . . . as you breathe their breath . . . feel their feelings . . .

(longer pause)

And perhaps even seeing you over there . . . with this pair of eyes . . . what you look like . . . sound like . . . how you seem . . . from this body . . . from this awareness . . . feeling what it feels like to be looking over at you, while breathing this breath . . . soft and easy . . . just allowing yourself the space to experience this . . . in the safe, magical space of the screen . . . with friendly but detached interest . . .

(longer pause)

And now . . . softly and easily . . . very gently wishing this body goodbye . . . with whatever thoughts and wishes you feel appropriate . . . saying goodbye to this other . . . and gently moving back into your own body . . . reinhabiting your own body . . . fully and easily . . . breathing deeply into your own belly . . . exhaling fully from your own nose and mouth . . .

And feeling grateful for your ability to move so easily here and there . . . you step out of the magical, translucent screen . . . back into your peaceful outdoor environment . . . again taking in the beautiful sights and sounds and smells . . . and watching the shimmering screen fade . . .

Understanding that you have in fact added to your own understanding in a very real way . . . increasing your own well-being as you open your mind and heart in this way . . . safely and easily . . . and knowing that you can do so again whenever you wish . . .

And so . . . very gently . . . and with soft eyes . . . coming back into the room whenever you are ready . . . knowing that you are better for this . . . and so you are . . .

SPIRITUAL IMAGERY

I want to repeat that spiritual imagery is in some ways a false category, in that all imagery is in some sense spiritual. What I'm calling spiritual imagery here is imagery that encourages us to experience a direct connection with the Divine, in whatever way that we experience divinity. This can be in the service of helping us with our view of ourselves, our connection to our own life or life's purpose, or in renewing our perception of ourselves as part of everyone and everything. In other words, this is imagery that can offer us perspective from the wider point of view of the mystic.

Spiritual Guide Imagery
(approximately 10 minutes)

To begin with, make yourself comfortable, positioning yourself so that your head, neck, and spine are straight . . . and shifting your weight so that your body feels fully supported . . .

And taking a couple of full, deep, cleansing breaths . . . inhaling as fully as you comfortably can . . . sending the warm energy of your breath to any part of your body that is sore or tense or tight . . . and releasing the discomfort with the exhale . . . so that you can feel your breath going to all the tight, tense places . . . loosening and softening them . . . and then, gathering up all the tension and breathing it out . . . so that more and more you can feel safe and comfortable, relaxed and easy, watching the cleansing action of the breath . . . with friendly but detached awareness . . .

And any distracting thoughts or feelings you might have . . . those, too, are sent out with the breath . . . so that inside you can be still and quiet . . . like a lake with no ripples . . .

And now, imagining a place where you feel safe and peaceful and easy . . . a place either make-believe or real . . . a place from your past . . . or somewhere you've always wanted to go . . . it doesn't matter . . . just so it's a place that feels good and safe and peaceful to you . . .

And allowing the place to become real to you . . . looking around you . . . taking the place in with your eyes . . . enjoying the colors . . . the scenery . . . looking over to your right . . . and over to your left . . .

And listening to the sounds of the place . . . whatever they might be . . . wind or water . . . the music of birds or crickets or a whole blend of sounds . . . the steady thrum of rain on a roof . . . just so your ears can become familiar with the sounds of the place . . .

And feeling whatever you are sitting against or lying upon . . . or perhaps feeling the quality of the ground beneath your feet . . . whether it's sand or pine needles or grass . . . or you might be in a cozy armchair . . . or sitting on a nice, warm rock in the sun . . .

And feeling the air on your skin . . . either brisk and breezy . . . or soft and still . . . crisp and dry . . . or balmy and wet . . . perhaps you are inside, feeling the warmth of a cozy fire on your face and hands . . . or maybe you are outdoors, and there's just the subtlest caress of a fragrant, gentle breeze . . . so just enjoying the feel of the place on your skin . . .

And smelling its rich fragrance . . . whether it's the soft, full scent of flowers . . . or the pungent smell of salt sea air . . . or sweet meadow grass . . .

And as you become more and more attuned to the safety and beauty of this place . . . feeling thankful and happy to be there . . . you begin to feel a kind *of a tingling on your skin . . . a pleasant, energizing something in the air . . . something that contains expectancy and excitement . . . and you know with some certainty . . . that it is good and right to be here . . . that there is magic in this place . . . and something wonderful is just about to happen . . .*

And as that certainty settles around you . . . you know to raise your eyes . . . and coming toward you . . . from very far away . . . you see a remarkable and shiny being . . . at first hard to distinguish . . . and then more and more discernible . . . emanating a full, soft aura of radiant light all around it . . . highlighting and intensifying everything it shines on . . .

And as this beautiful being approaches you . . . perhaps familiar . . . or perhaps not . . . maybe male or maybe female . . . or perhaps not a human form at all . . . it doesn't matter . . . just so you can feel the love and wisdom in the steady intensity of its beautiful light . . . approaching you . . .

(longer pause)

Coming up to you and bathing you in soft brightness . . . and feeling the light softly touch your skin . . . and letting it soak into you . . . deeper and deeper . . . permeating your body . . . as you experience the compassionate eyes looking at you . . . feeling the deep, kind gaze look into you . . .

Breathing this bright presence in . . . letting it move through you like a warm wave . . . understanding that you are being seen . . . seen in all your complexity . . . in all your simplicity . . . seen and understood and acknowledged . . . and just letting that awareness fill you . . .

Feeling your heart open to a warmth that expands into your entire chest . . . softly and easily . . . and all through your body . . . touching an ancient memory of who you really are . . . and who you have always been . . . and always will be . . . touching your own bright and indestructible soul . . . as you open to this sweet connection . . . enveloped in soft light . . . melting and merging and molding into it . . .

Held by the loving gaze of this beautiful being . . . held by deep understanding and a sense of utter safety . . . you can take in fully and deeply the love so freely offered to you . . . as you feel your own love in return . . . free and boundless . . . understanding that in this powerful circuitry between you, it is the same love that fills you both . . . that the giver is the receiver . . . and the receiver is the source . . .

So just taking a moment to experience the richness of the connection . . . and the boundless nature of your own open heart . . . feeling yourself grow larger in this exquisite energy . . . as your surroundings begin to sing and dance . . . glowing, sparkling, and vibrating in their own splendor . . .

Feeling a wonderful, peaceful kind of joy as you melt into the beauty of this light . . . dissolving boundaries and becoming part of the vibrance of your surroundings . . . becoming pure color . . . dancing energy . . . soaring song . . . one pulse with the planet . . . and with everything it supports and nourishes . . .

Seeing the beauty of your own life . . . and comprehending your own life's journey from the vantage of this powerful, healing light . . . seeing it all . . . all the pain and fear and hardship . . . all the courage and kindness and love . . . the special gifts and abilities . . . the moments of triumph and great beauty . . . the moments of despair and lost perspective . . . all of it . . . seen through the softness of this exquisite light . . .

And feeling a new kindness toward yourself and others . . . a new forgiveness of yourself and others for disappointments of the past . . . letting it go . . . letting it all go . . . making room for possibility and growth . . . for living the truth of who you really are . . . fulfilling your purpose . . . exquisitely attuned to this light . . . in harmony with all things . . . and feeling love and gratitude for this awareness . . .

Allowing yourself to just dwell here . . . for however long it feels right . . . and whenever it is time . . . letting your bright companion depart . . . just as smoothly and seamlessly as in coming to you . . . gently and easily moving on . . . going back to wherever it came from . . .

And so . . . feeling peaceful and easy . . . knowing you can call forth this beautiful being again . . . whenever you wish to . . . and still feeling the halo of powerful, loving light surrounding you . . . your own radiant, protective cushion . . .

Breathing rhythmically and easily . . . you can once again feel yourself in your beautiful surroundings . . . and feeling yourself in your body . . . fully present . . . aware of your skin . . . defining and protecting you . . . feeling safe and comfortable . . .

and perhaps enjoying the sensation of moving after being still for so long . . .

And so, gently and with soft eyes . . . letting yourself come back into the room whenever you are ready . . . knowing in a deep place that you are better for this . . .

And so you are . . .

CHAPTER 4

IMAGERY EXERCISES FOR EMOTIONAL RESILIENCY

Because imagery is so effective at shifting mood, cognition, and body sensation, it is a wonderful tool for fostering emotional resiliency and maintaining mental health. The mind and body are not separate entities. In fact, to even claim that they are *intimately connected* is misleading, because such a statement implies that they are separate. In fact, they are really *one and the same thing*. So imagery that is specifically geared to help with physical symptoms and body ailments will automatically help with mood and emotions at the same time.

All the imagery in this book, then, by definition, is imagery for emotional resiliency. Each and every exercise can boost self-esteem, foster a relaxed appreciation of self and others, and provide a kind of protective "emotional cushion" that slows down the psychic wear and tear of daily living. This is true whether you are listening to imagery that helps the body eliminate cancer cells or imagery that helps the psyche rinse and release grief. And because each and every imagery exercise in this book has elements that help settle people further down into their bodies and get more connected to their physical selves, they all serve to center, ground, and stabilize a stronger sense of self, regardless of the particular focus.

Clearly, some of the scripts that have already appeared in this book are especially geared to do this. For instance, the samples of what I've categorized as feeling-state imagery (Favorite Place Imagery, page 76, and Imagery to Reinhabit the Body, page 79) are designed to simply shift mood and help create a sense of emotional well-being. So, too, the energetic imagery (Energy Moving Imagery, page 86, and Walking Imagery Exercise, page 90) is particularly good for stabilizing psychological health.

The imagery used to demonstrate metaphoric imagery is adaptable to all manner of psychological issues (Transforming an Issue Located in the Body, page 105, and Transforming a Symbolic Issue on a Screen, page 110). The spiritual imagery (Spiritual Guide Imagery, page 128) also cushions the psyche and enhances emotional resiliency.*

The two imagery scripts characterized as psychological imagery (Imagery to Release Grief, page 116, and Imagery to Increase Empathy for Another, page 123) are two good examples of imagery used for emotional health, the first focusing on an internal issue and the second on an interpersonal one. In the pages that follow, I'll be provid-

---

*I get concerned with some of the spiritual imagery I have heard, where listeners are encouraged to get disconnected from their physical bodies (for instance, listeners are guided to soar up into the heavens, float among the stars, and so on), but then little is done to help them get back to earth and back into their bodies. I would argue very strongly that encouraging this split between body and spirit is not good for either emotional or physical health. Ideally, we want to *embody our spirits* and reintegrate these two aspects of the self.

ing you with a more complete sampling of psychological imagery.

In very simple terms, I'll be focusing on three basic things that we all need to be able to do in order to maintain our emotional resiliency and enhance our mental health. First, we need to be able to acknowledge and tolerate our own feelings, whatever they are. This keeps us in touch with ourselves, supplies us with vital data for our health and safety, and allows us to release the emotions we would otherwise be holding. And allowing our feelings gives us the gift of maximizing our energy, because none of it is lost or consumed in suppressing, holding, or denying the truth of them. This is the component that is *intrapersonal*, between us and our own inner selves.

Second, we need to feel safe (and in fact, *be* safe) by marshaling the protection of strong, healthy boundaries. Boundaries are what we use to distinguish where we end and others begin. Otherwise, we aren't able to protect ourselves from others, and we run the risk of violating others, sometimes without even knowing it. This is the *interpersonal* component, the territory between ourselves and others.

And finally, we need to increase our general self-esteem by better understanding and appreciating who we really are and what we have to give to the world. This usually means seeing ourselves from a larger perspective, with more loving—and I would say more accurate—eyes than our usual nearsighted ones. With self-esteem comes the motivation and empowerment to express who we are and what we have to give. Ultimately, self-esteem is about connecting more fully to our sense of purpose and our life's meaning. So this component is about our *relationship to the world at large*.

IMAGERY TO HELP TOLERATE FEELINGS

Emotionally we can be far more resilient if we can allow ourselves to experience our feelings without criticism or blame. To fully know who we are, we need to experience what we feel. To have all our energy available to us, we need to experience what we feel. And we need to experience what we feel in order to properly protect ourselves.

Criticism and blame tend to interfere with this process of experiencing our feelings. We are all filled with "shoulds" and "should nots" about our emotions. We shouldn't feel angry, frightened, jealous, or spiteful. We should feel loving, cheerful, generous, and forgiving. The problem with this is simple: Much as we might try, we can't control or deny our feelings—our behavior, yes, but our feelings, no. They are what they are. And the price of denying them—at least over time—is a sense of emptiness, anxiety, or depression, or all three. We cannot authentically change our feelings into something more "acceptable" to us until we first acknowledge what they are and *own* them. Because a real paradox operates here: The more we disown, deny, and hold ourselves apart from our feelings, the more stubbornly stuck they stay to us. And the more we can soften around them, accept them, and allow them to just be, the more likely they are to flow on out of us, of their own accord, exactly the way they were meant to do. If we're human, we're going to experience the whole gamut of emotions. An insistence on feeling just the "nice" ones, because of our misplaced moral judgments, will, paradoxically, make them less accessible to us.

Denying feelings is the same as lying to ourselves. At some level, our true self knows the truth, and so we are split off from ourselves. When we disconnect from the truth of ourselves, we are cutting ourselves off from our very life force, and we are in fact weaker, less energized, and less focused than we could be. In fact, we could define depression as *the absence of a connection to our feelings, a blockage between ourselves and our emotions.* Take a look at the flattened, weary face of any clinically depressed person and you'll see how true this is.*

So, too, a full-blown anxiety attack is initially generated, psychodynamically speaking, by the rumblings of suppressed feelings that just don't want to stay down. Rather than let them come up, which feels wrong or dangerous in some way, the psyche sits on them harder. The tension from this inner battle finally erupts as a sudden, intense experience of anxiety. And, as the thousands of people who suffer from severe anxiety or phobias know all too well, over time anxiety can take on a life of its own and become hard to extinguish. But in the beginning, it is simply the inner self saying, "No more denying these feelings!" So at the psyche's simplest level, we can say that both depression and anxiety are a function of denying feelings. It's a learned behavior, not a natural one, and it usually comes from having been taught negative judgments about them.

I'm not dismissing the need for moral judgments; but we need them to help us assess and control *our behavior, not our feelings.* Action is an appropriate, sensible place for us to apply our ideas of right and wrong. And we can, in fact, do a better job of "doing right" when we can freely examine and assess what we feel, without editing out the parts we consider to be bad or shameful.

*Sometimes people say they are depressed when what they really mean is that they are sad. Being sad is nothing like being depressed. When we are sad, we are connected to our feelings, and this is inherently good and healthful. Although depression will have components of sadness, disappointment, and anger woven into it, it is primarily characterized by emotional flatness, loss of energy, and self-hatred.

Imagery can help us accept, acknowledge, and release our feelings. Even the most rigidly defended psyche will eventually soften and relent with repeated listening to imagery. Try this next exercise to help you identify, acknowledge, and shift any emotions you might have.

You'll probably notice that this imagery focuses on *what the feelings are like*, as opposed to *why they are there*. This keeps you out of your head (the cognitive, analytic left side of your brain) and encourages you to stay in your experience, your body, and your experiential right brain. For our purposes, this is where the healing is: not in asking the question "Why is this?" which is the question that the left side of the brain always wants answered, but in asking "What is this?"* So use this imagery to connect into your feelings, and consider it to be good, preventive medicine for keeping anxiety and depression from your doorstep.

Imagery to Connect with Feelings
(approximately 10 minutes)

Please position yourself as comfortably as you can, shifting your weight so your body can be fully supported. See if you can arrange it so your head, neck, and spine are straight and aligned.

And taking a full, deep, cleansing breath . . . (pause) . . . exhaling as fully as you comfortably can . . . (pause) . . . and again . . . taking another breath . . . deep into the belly . . . (pause) . . .

---

*Of course, there are many times when the left-brain, rational way of problem solving is exactly what is needed. But there are times when this can have you going around in circles, covering the same bases again and again and coming up with nothing. This is when it particularly makes sense to launch a right-brain approach to the same problem.

*and breathing out . . . fully and comfortably . . .
(pause) . . .*

*And gently turning your attention inward . . .
focusing inside for just this next while . . . to see
how you feel inside your body . . . just a gentle,
curious inventory of how you are doing in there . . .*

*Interested in your own well-being . . . looking
into how you are at this moment . . . sensing your
energy level . . . your mood . . . your sense of physical well-being . . . continuing to breathe deeply and
easily . . . looking with a friendly, curious eye . . .
with detached, neutral interest . . .*

*And feeling the places inside your body where you
might be tight or tense or sore . . . and where you
might feel soft, relaxed, and open . . . so just letting
your awareness move around inside your body . . .
with friendly but detached interest . . .*

*Starting perhaps with your head . . . checking to
see how it feels inside your head . . . whether it
seems tight and congested . . . or comfortable and
open . . .*

(longer pause)

*And moving down into your neck and shoulders
. . . curious about how it feels in there . . .
(pause) . . .*

*And down into your heart . . . continuing to
breathe deeply and easily . . . sensing how it feels
around your heart . . . noticing any heaviness or
tightness there . . . with friendly but detached interest . . . no praise, no blame . . . (pause) . . .*

140

And checking to see how your whole chest feels . . . (pause) . . . moving your awareness around to your back . . . (pause) . . . checking out the entire length of your back . . . (pause) . . . and moving around to the belly . . . looking to see what it feels like in there . . . continuing to breathe deeply and easily . . . noting with friendly but detached interest any tension or tightness in the belly . . . (pause) . . .

And moving your awareness down into your bottom . . . seeing how it feels along your whole pelvic floor . . . (pause) . . .

And down into your legs . . . feeling any tightness or rigidity in the legs . . . all the way down to your feet . . . all the way down to the tips of your toes . . .

Just doing this gentle, curious inventory . . . no praise, no blame . . . just curious to see what is . . . for the sake of your own well-being . . .

And now, breathing into the very center of your body . . . wherever you sense that to be . . . (pause) . . . and breathing out . . . (pause) . . . and again . . . deep into the very center of your body . . . (pause) . . . and exhaling fully and easily . . . (pause) . . .

And asking your body to show you what it's feeling . . . and leaving space open for it to answer . . . breathing in very easily . . . open and steady and clear . . . asking your feelings to show themselves to you . . . and breathing out, fully and easily . . . asking to see where they are held in the body . . . staying open and curious to sense their location . . . and what these emotions look and feel like . . . so just letting the intelligence of the body show them to you . . .

Clearing away a space . . . and letting the wisdom of the body answer . . . showing you a place that might be denser, heavier than the rest . . . perhaps a soft sadness around the heart . . . or maybe a vibrating, scared feeling in the belly . . . maybe it's a feeling of excitement and joy, so big you feel confined inside your own skin . . . or perhaps you find yourself holding tight to a clenched anger in your legs . . . whatever it is you might be feeling . . . wherever it is . . . just letting it begin to reveal itself to you . . . and allowing yourself to acknowledge what is there . . . however subtle and elusive . . . knowing you can be curious and neutral . . . detached and easy . . . an intrepid explorer of your own inner territory . . .

And with another deep, full breath . . . ready to take a closer look at this feeling or mix of feelings . . . and breathing out fully and easily . . . going to wherever it sits . . . curious about the texture of it . . . (pause) . . . the size of it . . . (pause) . . . the feel of it . . . (pause) . . . so just granting yourself the space to investigate more fully . . . into its nature . . . its intensity . . . whatever colors it might have . . . (pause) . . . or sounds . . . (pause) . . . or tastes . . . (pause) . . . or smells . . . (pause) . . . so that you're moving your awareness all around and through it . . . to whatever degree it feels comfortable . . . in your own way . . . and your own time . . .

(longer pause)

And asking the body to continue to show you whatever you need to know about this . . . trusting it to reveal what you need to see . . . as you continue to breathe deeply and easily . . . all around and through this feeling . . . no praise, no blame . . . just a friendly but detached interest . . .

Able to trust this process of knowing yourself better . . . of connecting more deeply with yourself . . . and so giving yourself all the room that you need . . . to let the energy of these feelings begin to shift and move inside you . . .

And should the mind start to judge or analyze or overthink . . . just turning your attention back to the experience of your feelings . . . knowing there will be a time when all of this will make sense to you . . . and it doesn't have to be now . . . that this is a time for simply experiencing what is there . . .

And so . . . taking whatever time you need . . . continuing to breathe deeply and easily . . . grateful for your capacity for self-awareness . . . and saluting your own courage . . . whenever you are ready . . . coming back into the room . . . gently and with soft eyes . . . knowing you are better for this . . .

And so you are . . .

IMAGERY TO ALLEVIATE DEPRESSION

Most psychotherapists believe there are many possible reasons for depression. One is that we haven't been so successful at staying in tune with uncomfortable feelings; another is that life may have conspired to place us in circumstances that leave us feeling so trapped, powerless, and hopeless that our defense is to anesthetize ourselves and sleepwalk through the day; still another is that we've inherited a biochemical imbalance in our bodies. Although all of these things are usually present in depression, I'm not sure the links are so clearly causal. It could be that these things are simply the concomitant features of depression, and they feed on each other.

In any case, I want to focus on how depression is *experienced*, because I think that will be the most useful perspective for our purposes. And mostly, depression is experienced as the *absence of feelings*. Very depressed people come by their characteristically flat, deadened facial appearance and immobilizing fatigue honestly enough— quite simply, there is a barrier between them and their feelings. Feelings are energy. When feelings can't be accessed, generic energy is blocked as well. Even mild depression has this quality of physical and emotional "energylessness."*

Imagery can help release some of that trapped energy, especially if the depression is not too severe. Severe depression, like anxiety, can take on a life of its own and is hard to alleviate with imagery alone. Sometimes a combination of psychotherapy, medication, a change in diet and exercise habits, and various body-mind techniques, including imagery, is needed. Acting in concert, they can interrupt and reverse the downward spiral.

All of us have times of feeling depressed as part of normal living. The imagery that follows is especially geared to this kind of normal-range depression and is designed to release blocked energy, reestablish a connection

*The typical characteristics of depression are loss of energy, flattened mood, poor concentration, memory loss, irritability, feelings of hopelessness and helplessness, more than usual self-criticism, and a cognitive distortion about how bad things really are— everything is seen through a very dark lens. When it's associated with anxiety, it's called an agitated depression. More serious depressions are accompanied by disturbed sleep patterns and loss of appetite. People should get professional help if they're struggling with most of these symptoms and getting nowhere.

with inner feelings, and interrupt the hopelessness and self-hatred that, above all else, are the signature of depression, even the short-lived kind.

Because the imagery is designed to help access and balance emotional energy, it is also helpful for people who are suffering from anxiety. In fact, many bouts of depression are accompanied by anxiety, so people are frequently dealing with the discomforts of both anyway.

The depression imagery that follows starts with the mood-altering Favorite Place Imagery, introduced in Chapter 3, to create a relaxed, altered state from which the imagery can be experienced. To help overcome the isolating and dispiriting effects of depression, powerful images of a mystical cone of light and potent spiritual assistance help set up the release of core energy that follows.

*Depression Imagery**

(approximately 14 minutes)

Please get yourself comfortable . . . shifting your weight so you're allowing your body to be fully supported . . . and your head, neck, and spine are aligned . . .

And taking a couple of deep, full, cleansing breaths, inhaling as fully as you comfortably can . . . sending the warm energy of your breath to any part of your body that's sore or tense or tight . . . and releasing the discomfort with the exhale . . . so that

---

*Taken from the *Health Journeys* guided imagery tape *For People with Depression*, Time Warner AudioBooks, Los Angeles, California, 1993 *you can feel your breath going to all the tight, tense places . . . loosening and softening them . . . and then gathering up all the tension and breathing it out . . . so that more and more you can feel safe and comfortable, relaxed and easy, watching the cleansing action of the breath . . . with friendly but detached awareness . . .*

And now . . . imagining a place where you feel safe and peaceful and easy . . . a place either real or imaginary . . . a place from your past . . . or somewhere that you've always wanted to go . . . it doesn't matter . . . just so it is a place that feels good and safe and peaceful to you . . .

And allowing the place to become more real to you . . . looking around you . . . taking the place in with your eyes . . . enjoying the colors . . . the scenery . . . looking over to your right . . . and over to your left . . .

And listening to the sounds of the place . . . whatever they might be . . . wind or water . . . birds or crickets or a whole blend of sounds . . . just so your ears can enjoy the unique music of your special place . . .

And feeling whatever you are sitting against or lying upon . . . or perhaps feeling the quality of the ground beneath your feet . . . whether it's sand or pine needles or grass . . . perhaps you're in a cozy armchair . . . or sitting on a nice, warm rock in the sun . . .

And feeling the air on your skin . . . either crisp and dry . . . or balmy and wet . . . perhaps you are indoors, feeling the warmth of a cozy fire on your face and hands . . . or maybe you are outside, and there's just the subtlest caress of a fragrant, gentle breeze on your face . . . so just enjoying the feel of the place on your skin . . .

And smelling its rich fragrance . . . whether it's the soft, full scent of flowers . . . or sharp, salt sea air . . . sweet meadow grass . . . or maybe the pungent smell of peat moss on the forest floor . . .

And as you become more and more attuned to the safety and beauty of this place . . . feeling thankful and happy to be there . . . you begin to feel a kind of tingling . . . a pleasant, energizing something in the air . . . something that contains expectancy and excitement . . . a sense that something wonderful is just about to happen . . .

And as that certainty settles around you, you notice that the tingling is taking on a kind of a glow . . . that the air is alive with vibrant energy . . .

And from somewhere above you, a cone of powerful white light is softly and steadily moving down . . . forming a tent of vibrant tingling energy all around you . . . surrounding and protecting you . . . illuminating everything it touches with exquisite brightness . . . highlit definition . . . vibrating color . . . giving everything it shines on a fresh, new beauty . . .

You can feel the air around you intensifying, glowing, dancing with sparkling energy . . . and with a sense of gentle wonder for such stunning beauty . . . you feel the tingling energy of the light

*moving down into your body . . . softly entering
your head and neck . . . warming your shoulders
. . . feeling the muscle subtly soften, release, and
expand . . .*

*Gently penetrating into your chest . . . and mov-
ing into the heaviness around the heart . . . slowly
and easily . . . softly massaging and opening . . .
moving all around the edges of the heaviness . . .
steadily kneading and softening and releasing . . .*

*And continuing down the spine . . . filling your
back and torso . . . penetrating into the layers of
tissue . . . deeper and deeper . . . slowly and steadily
moving into every organ . . . cleansing and clearing . . .*

*Sending a warm, vibrating softness into the weari-
ness in the belly . . . gently warming and opening
. . . soft and easy . . . filling it with the powerful,
healing energy of the light . . .*

*Working its magic deep inside your body . . .
moving with deliberate intelligence to the hidden
places where pain and disappointment are stored . . .
right to the center of the heaviness . . . and feeling
the spaces loosen and lighten as you breathe into them
. . . sensing the beginnings of energy awakening
. . . old sparks returning . . .*

*You gradually become aware that you are not
alone . . . that there is a warm presence all around
you . . . and looking around . . . surprised but not
surprised . . . you see that you are surrounded by
gentle, loving beings . . . immediately recognizable
as allies . . . smiling and nodding in the soft beauty*

*of the light . . . some perhaps familiar . . . or per-
haps not . . . but all warming you with their protective presence . . .*

*One of them softly approaches you . . . and with
a wonderful, deep, gentle look, directly into your
eyes . . . gently touches the center of your chest . . .
with a warm, gentle touch . . . sending a charge of
gentle but powerful energy directly into your heart
. . . strong waves of nourishing, vital energy . . .
moving right through barriers of dull, deadened space
. . . melting away the thick, heavy fog . . . releasing
and awakening the core energies beneath . . . and
you can feel the energy begin to spiral . . . wider
and wider . . . charging and renewing each and every
cell . . .*

*So just letting yourself feel the stirrings of your
own energy . . . as it starts to bubble up, simmer,
and roll to a boil, deep in your center . . . sensing
your own unique, vital life force . . . pulsing and
vibrating . . . radiating strength and purpose to every corner of your being . . .*

*You see in the eyes that are looking at you that
they see what you see . . . that you are healing . . .
that you are remembering your own vitality and
aliveness . . . that you can feel it deep inside you
. . . breathing in to touch it . . . (pause) . . . breathing out to let it move through you . . . (pause) . . .
deep, full, nourishing breaths . . .*

*And suddenly you know with your whole heart
. . . with your whole being . . . that you are healing
. . . that you will continue to heal . . . that the
heaviness will continue to lighten . . . that the fog*

you've been trapped in will continue to burn away in the bright, humming light . . . as more and more you are able to release the places where feelings are held . . . breathing out pain and tiredness . . . (pause) . . . breathing in the beauty of the dancing light . . . (pause) . . . and releasing sadness and despair with the out breath . . . (pause) . . . taking in joy and hope with the in breath . . . (pause) . . . and breathing out resentment and pain . . .

Knowing you are healing . . . feeling your heart expand and open to its own vastness . . . attuned once more to the brightness of your own being . . . and the generosity of your spirit . . . breathing in to touch it . . . (pause) . . . and breathing out to send it all through you . . . (pause) . . .

The special one says to you, "Remember, we are always here . . . it is you who come and go . . . call for us anytime and we will come . . . to help you heal . . . to help you remember who you really are" . . . and gathering up a handful of the glowing, vibrating light . . . gives it to you for safekeeping . . . your own special supply, to use as needed . . .

And with a special look of deep understanding . . . bows and fades away with the others . . .

And so : . . . feeling peaceful and easy . . . you watch as the light slowly begins to withdraw . . . returning to wherever it came from . . . until it is gone altogether . . . for now . . . knowing it is yours to call forth whenever you wish . . .

And once again, you see yourself in your safe and peaceful outdoor surroundings . . . feeling safe and relaxed and easy . . . although perhaps the colors around you are brighter . . . the sounds more vivid . . . the air more alive . . .

You might feel that something powerful has happened . . . that a major shift has occurred . . . and will continue to occur . . . with or without your conscious working on it . . .

And you see very clearly that you can call forth this place . . . the light . . . the magical band of allies . . . whenever you wish to further the work that you have already done . . .

And so . . . feeling yourself sitting in your chair . . . or lying down . . . breathing in and out . . . very rhythmically and easily . . . gently and with soft eyes . . . coming back into the room whenever you are ready . . . knowing in a deep place that you are better for this . . .

And so you are . . .

IMAGERY TO ENCOURAGE HEALTHY BOUNDARIES

One of the signs of solid mental health is when we can distinguish ourselves from others, and know where our own borders are. This helps us protect ourselves from inappropriate invasions of our space—either physical or emotional—by others. It also protects others from us, because we can recognize *their* inviolable space and keep out of it.

I can recall a fairly harmless example of missing the mark in the boundary department from my own family. I remember my mother admonishing me, time and time again, to "Wear a sweater! You're cold!" This would be accompanied by her folding her arms tightly to her chest and shivering. Invariably, my irritated adolescent reply would be, "No, Ma, *you're* cold—*you* wear a sweater!" (Teenagers are famous for their prickly boundaries—individuation is their developmental job, after all.) My mother was doing what we therapists call projection, which was taking what she felt and assigning it to me. Even emotionally healthy people like my mother can be frequently sighted projecting onto those they love. Usually, they will pull back and reestablish who is who. But psychologically fragile people will project all kinds of feelings onto many people a great deal of the time, and won't know they're doing it. This can make the world a pretty confusing place for them—and for those around them, too.

An even more worrisome form of boundary weakness is when someone has such permeable "edges" that they are too much at the mercy of their environment. This is the person who leaves the house in a wonderful mood, runs into a depressed friend who is having a bad day, and walks away from that encounter feeling terrible. Picking up everyone else's feelings—even when the feelings are euphoric—is not a good idea. *We need to be having our own feelings, not someone else's.* And although it's desirable to be empathic and sensitive to others, it shouldn't be at the exorbitant price of losing our own sense of inner reality.

The most extreme form of boundary difficulty is in relationships where abuse happens, from the point of view of both the one who abuses and the one who is abused. People who have been abused often don't recognize when their boundaries are being violated, because they've been acclimatized to inappropriate intrusion. The intactness of their edges has been compromised, and they lack an awareness of their own inviolate inner space. (Fortunately, there are many wonderful and psychologically inexplicable exceptions to this general statement.) And abusers, too, from their end of the equation, lack a sense of their victim's *otherness*, usually because of the broken boundaries they themselves experienced from their own history of abuse.

So all of this is to say that boundaries are a good thing to have. Certainly, we don't want them to be so thick and rigid that we are rendered heartless, isolated, and untouched by other people and their circumstances. But we do need to be able to consciously elect to open and close ours, and choose to let things in or keep things out as we see fit. And always, *always*, we must be able to touch back into ourselves and our own inner experience.

The imagery that follows has many components to it, all designed to enhance healthy boundaries. Some of the imagery reinforces the perception of a protective cushion of energy around each of us. Some of it keys us back into a sense of feeling loved, safe, and protected. And finally, some of it refocuses our attention back into ourselves, to the core that our boundaries are serving to protect.

Imagery for Healthy Boundaries
(approximately 12 minutes)

Please arrange it so that you're comfortable, either sitting or lying down with your head, neck, and spine straight. Feel free to move around and adjust your body, until you feel fully supported by whatever is supporting you . . .

And taking a deep, full, cleansing breath . . . (pause) . . . exhaling as fully as you comfortably can . . . (pause) . . . and another . . . breathing deep into the belly, if you can . . . expanding the entire abdomen . . . (pause) . . . and again, breathing out as fully and completely as you can . . .

And once more . . . breathing in and sending the warm energy of the breath to any part of your body that's tense or sore or tight . . . and releasing the tension with the exhale . . . so you can feel your breath going to all the tight, tense places . . . loosening and softening them . . . and then, gathering up all the tension and breathing it out . . . so that more and more you can feel safe and peaceful and easy . . . watching the cleansing action of the breath . . .

And any unwelcome thoughts that come to mind . . . those, too, can be sent out with the breath . . . released with the exhale . . . so that for just a moment, the mind is empty . . . for just a split second, it is free and clear space, and you are blessed with stillness . . .

And any emotions that are rocking around in there . . . those, too, can be noted, acknowledged, and sent out with the breath . . . so that your emotional self can be still and quiet . . . like a lake with no ripples . . .

And now, if you would focus your attention inward . . . to see how your body is feeling . . . to take a gentle, curious inventory of your insides . . .

Looking into where it feels tight or tense or sore . . . and where it feels loose and soft and open . . .

letting your awareness move around inside your body . . . with the neutral, clear detached eye of a camera . . .

And perhaps checking to see what your energy level is like . . . how your mood is . . . no praise, no blame . . . just a friendly but detached interest in how you are feeling . . .

Continuing to breathe fully and easily . . . as you move your awareness all through your body . . . starting perhaps with your head . . . checking to see how it feels inside your head . . . (pause) . . .

And moving down into your neck and shoulders . . . curious about any tightness or heaviness there . . . (pause) . . .

And into your chest . . . continuing to breathe smoothly and deeply . . . sensing how it feels around your heart . . . (pause) . . . aware of any sensation there . . . heavy or tight . . . or spacious or filled . . . (pause) . . .

Moving around into the length of the back . . . noting how your back feels all along your spine . . . (pause) . . . all the way to your tailbone . . . (pause) . . .

And coming back around . . . seeing how it feels in your belly . . . continuing to breathe deeply and easily . . . feeling what is happening all through your abdomen . . . no praise, no blame . . . just noticing in a friendly but detached way any tension or fear that might be held there . . . (pause) . . .

And moving your awareness down into your bottom . . . seeing how it feels along your whole pelvic floor . . .

And down into your legs . . . feeling any tightness or rigidity in the legs . . . (pause) . . . all the way down to the feet . . . all the way to the tips of your toes . . .

Just taking this space to reacquaint yourself with this body of yours . . . your steadiest companion . . . your oldest friend . . . listening to it . . . acknowledging it . . .

And letting your awareness sink down into it . . . settling your spirit down into your body . . . letting it fill all your inner spaces . . . all the way down to the tips of your fingers and toes . . . with the soft, easy, rolling motion of a rich, misty fog . . .

Continuing to breathe fully and deeply . . . in and out . . . (pause) . . . fully inhabiting your body . . . feeling more and more the comfort of being home . . .

And now, if you would . . . bringing your notice to the feel of the air immediately around you . . . aware of where it touches your skin . . . and allowing yourself to feel the remarkable boundary of your skin . . . (pause) . . . and the feel of the air and your clothes on it . . . (pause) . . .

And perhaps beginning to perceive something immediately around you . . . a vibrating cushion of energy . . . surrounding and protecting you . . . and so you can begin to sense the layers that you have . . . your spirit, nestled deeply and comfortably in your body . . . and this bright cushion of energy . . . surrounding your body . . .

And with another full, deep breath . . . (pause) . . . sending your breath out into this cushion . . . the energy of the out breath adding to its density and size . . . and again . . . breathing in . . . (pause) . . . and with the exhale, extending it out even further . . . (pause) . . .

Making more and more palpable this protective cushion of energy . . . feeling it tingle and vibrate all around you . . . while inside, you can feel safe and protected . . . relaxed and easy . . . able to take in what is nourishing to you . . . but insulated from what you don't want or need . . .

Continuing to send the powerful energy of the breath out into it . . . infusing it with your spirit . . . adding even further to its fullness . . . understanding that this is part of who you are . . . and just taking a moment to feel it around you . . . (pause) . . .

And now . . . see if you can imagine that this cushion of energy is drawing to it all the love and sweetness that has ever been felt for you by anyone at any time . . . feeling it pull in all the caring and loving kindness that has ever been sent your way . . . every prayer and good wish, permeating and filling the field of energy surrounding you . . . pulling it all in like a powerful magnet . . . calling every good wish home . . . and so increasing the powerful, protective field around you even further . . .

And perhaps even sensing the presence of all those who have ever loved or nurtured you . . .

the ones you want with you . . . sensing them around you now . . . people or places . . . perhaps even seeing fleeting glimpses of them . . . or maybe just feeling them there . . . those who believed in you . . . loved and protected you . . . or guided you well . . . people from your life . . . alive or long gone . . . or perhaps special animals, guardian angels, or magical beings . . . it doesn't matter . . . just so you feel their protection and support . . .

And so continuing to breathe, fully and deeply . . . sensing the protection around you . . . soft and rich and full . . . at your service . . . yours to keep with you . . . or to call to your side whenever you wish . . .

As you stay in the center of your body . . . strong and steady . . . fully present . . . comfortably home in your body . . . safe and protected . . .

And so . . . whenever you are ready . . . coming back into the room . . . strong, resilient, and relaxed . . . knowing you are better for this . . .

And so you are . . .

IMAGERY FOR SELF-ESTEEM

Although all the imagery in this book and this chapter can enhance self-esteem, the exercise that follows addresses it specifically. The script is designed to increase understanding, empathy, and appreciation for yourself. Perhaps that sounds self-indulgent. But I'm not talking about the kind of brittle, shallow self-puffery that we associate with bragging and phony self-aggrandizement. Rather, this is the kind of compassionate, genuine appreciation that *everyone* deserves. And the truth of the matter is, in most cases, if we don't have this for ourselves, we'll be short on it with others. (And unfortunately, the reverse is also true: If we tend to be harsh and critical with ourselves, we usually extend *that* to others as well.)

Because a fresh view of the self is not so easy to come by, several steps are used in this imagery to gradually lead you into it—the favorite place and the device of the screen. The core image involves getting you to see yourself, almost literally, with someone else's eyes—someone much kinder than you!

Imagery to See Yourself with Kinder Eyes
(approximately 14 minutes)

To begin with, see if you can position yourself as comfortably as you can, shifting your weight so you're allowing your body to be fully supported . . . with your head, neck, and spine aligned . . .

And taking a couple of deep, cleansing breaths, inhaling as fully as you comfortably can . . . sending the warm energy of your breath to any part of your body that's sore or tense or tight . . . and releasing the discomfort with the exhale . . . so that you can feel your breath going to all the tight, tense places . . . loosening and softening them . . . and then gathering up all the tension . . . and breathing it out . . . so that more and more you can feel safe and comfortable, relaxed and easy, watching the cleansing action of the breath . . . with friendly but detached awareness . . .

And any unwelcome thoughts or feelings you might have . . . those, too, are sent out with the breath . . . so that inside you can be still and quiet . . . like a lake with no ripples . . .

And now, imagining a place . . . inside or outdoors . . . where you feel safe and peaceful and easy . . . a place either make-believe or real . . . a place from your past . . . or somewhere that you've always wanted to go . . . it doesn't matter . . . just so it is a place that feels good and safe and peaceful to you . . .

(longer pause)

And allowing the place to become real to you . . . looking around you . . . taking the place in with your eyes . . . enjoying the colors . . . the scenery . . . appreciating every detail with your eyes . . . looking over to your right . . . and over to your left . . .

And listening to the sounds of the place . . . the music of moving wind or water . . . birds or crickets . . . soft night sounds . . . perhaps the steady thrumming of rain on the roof . . . it doesn't matter . . . just so your ears can enjoy the sounds of your place . . . that is so safe and peaceful to you . . .

And feeling whatever you are sitting against or lying upon . . . or perhaps feeling the quality of the ground beneath your feet . . . whether it's sand or pine needles or grass . . . or you might be in a cozy armchair . . . or sitting on a nice, warm rock in the sun . . .

And feeling the air on your skin . . . either brisk and breezy . . . or soft and still . . . crisp and dry . . . or balmy and wet . . . or perhaps you are indoors, feeling the warmth of a cozy fire on your face and hands . . . or maybe you are outdoors, and there's just the subtlest caress of a fragrant, gentle breeze . . . so just enjoying the feel of the place on your skin . . .

And smelling its rich fragrance . . . whether it's the soft, full scent of flowers . . . or the sharpness of salt sea air . . . sweet meadow grass . . . or the pungent smell of peat moss in the forest . . .

And as you become more and more attuned to the safety and beauty of this place . . . feeling thankful and happy to be there . . . you begin to feel a kind of tingling . . . a pleasant energizing something in the air all around you . . . something that contains expectancy and excitement . . . a sense that something wonderful is just about to happen . . .

And as you look out in front of you . . . you begin to discern that there is a kind of transparent screen shimmering there . . . getting more and more opaque and solid as you look at it . . .

And as you watch the screen . . . with a kind of peaceful curiosity . . . you gradually become aware of a form beginning to appear on it . . . becoming more and more defined . . . and you realize that this is the form of a very special someone . . . perhaps it

161

*is someone who loved you well from your past . . .
maybe a special guide or teacher . . . a parent or
grandparent . . . maybe someone who once loved
you very much . . . or someone in your life still . . .*

*It could also be an angel or spirit or special-power
animal . . . it doesn't matter . . . just so it's someone
or something that you know is good and wise and
kind and loving . . . with the ability to see from the
heart into the truth of things . . . deeply and clearly
. . . (pause) . . .*

*So you watch, as this special someone or something
becomes more and more defined on the screen . . .
until the three-dimensional image is quite clear . . .
in whatever characteristic posture they have . . .
wearing whatever it is that they wear . . . doing
whatever it is that they do . . . crisp and clear in
every dimension . . .*

(longer pause)

*And you can softly and easily enter the screen . . .
feeling yourself drawn to them . . . wanting to have
a closer look . . . undetected by them, you can slip
into the screen . . . safely and easily . . . able to
have a slow, respectful walk around them . . . seeing
them from every angle . . . the expression on the
face . . . (pause) . . . the profile and the back . . .
(pause) . . . and sensing the feel of the air around
them . . . the special energy surrounding them . . .
(pause) . . . the sounds of the breathing or the voice
. . . (pause) . . . the scent in the air around them
. . . (pause) . . . so just slowly moving around them
. . . pleased to experience a full, rich sensory awareness of them . . .*

And now . . . in the magical, safe space of the screen . . . somehow, for just a short while . . . sliding past the boundaries and slipping into the body of this other being . . . entering this other body and breathing their breath . . . for just a brief while . . .

And if there is any resistance to doing this . . . just gently noting it . . . and allowing yourself to soften all around it . . . for the sake of understanding more . . . and learning what you need to know . . . just an experiment . . . breathing their breath . . . looking down and seeing this other body . . . perhaps other hands or feet or clothing . . .

Breathing deeply into this other being . . . and sensing the feelings . . . whatever they are . . . (pause) . . . perhaps a sense of warmth and peace and calm . . . or a soft expansion around the heart . . . maybe a solid, steady sense of safety and security . . . whatever feelings or sensations . . . just experiencing what it feels like in the chest and belly . . . in the muscles, skin, and bone . . . staying open and curious as to how it feels inside this other body . . .

And seeing out from their eyes . . . what the world looks like . . . sounds like . . . feels like . . . as you breathe with their breath . . . feel with their feelings . . . soft and easy . . . feeling their heart beating inside you . . . steady and calm . . .

(longer pause)

And perhaps even seeing you over there . . . with these other eyes . . . looking over at you . . . and seeing who you really are . . . looking under,

163

around, and through your surface . . . to the essence of who you really are . . . and seeing all the hidden splendor . . . all the vast beauty of your being . . .

(longer pause)

And perhaps seeing what you are here to do . . . with all your unique gifts and special abilities . . . appreciating what you were born to do . . . in your own way . . . in your own time . . .

And so just taking a moment to experience this . . . gently and easily . . . with all the focus you can bring to bear . . .

(longer pause)

And now . . . very softly and easily . . . whenever you are ready . . . wishing this body, this awareness goodbye . . . in whatever way feels right . . . (pause) . . . and still infused with the richness of this experience . . . still feeling the expanded energy in your heart . . . very gently moving back into your own body . . . reinhabiting it fully and easily . . . breathing into it with your own breath . . . through your own nose and mouth . . . back home . . . connected again to your body, your steadiest companion and your oldest friend . . .

And sliding out of the magical, translucent screen . . . and once again see yourself in your safe and peaceful special surroundings . . . again taking in its beautiful sights and sounds and smells . . .

And watching as the screen fades away . . . and feeling yourself in the chair . . . breathing very

STAYING WELL WITH GUIDED IMAGERY

*rhythmically and easily . . . very gently and with
soft eyes . . . allowing yourself to come back into the
room whenever you are ready . . . knowing in a
deep place you are better for this . . .*

And so you are . . .

CHAPTER 5

IMAGERY EXERCISES FOR COMMON COMPLAINTS

Imagery can be a big help with headaches, allergies, insomnia, pain, and other commonplace problems. Of course, you will always want to check out worrisome symptoms with your doctor. But once you've been reassured that nothing terrible is going on, you can feel free to experiment and see whether imagery alone is enough to reduce your discomfort, or whether it makes sense to use it in concert with medicine or other kinds of interventions. And, as always, use your own imagination, common sense, and resourcefulness to flesh out whatever I offer here so that the imagery meets you on your own unique ground.

IMAGERY TO ALLEVIATE HEADACHE

After general pain, headache is the symptom we vulnerable humans are most likely to get. Typically, a headache will come from stress, overdoing it with food or alcohol, from tobacco, flu, allergy, colds, eyestrain, or muscle strain. More severe and less likely causes are head injury, brain abscess, meningitis, and brain tumor. If you have a headache that lasts longer than twenty-four hours, one that recurs two or three times a week, or one that is associated with nausea, vomiting, or drowsiness, you need to see your doctor.*

The headache imagery that I offer you here is for the standard, garden-variety nuisance headache, the kind that you get from tension; from overeating or drinking too much alcohol or caffeine; from quickly taking yourself off alcohol or caffeine; from colds or flu; neck strain or eyestrain; missing a meal; hormone changes around menstruation; or exposure to strong sunlight, stuffy surroundings, or excessive noise. These headaches are annoying but essentially harmless, and if you were to do nothing, they would go away by themselves sooner or later. This imagery is designed to encourage them to go away sooner.

Physiologically, we can boil down what produces a headache to one of two things. The first is muscle strain from tension in the facial, neck, or scalp muscles (tension headache). The second is from strain within the walls of the blood vessels in the head (vascular headache), either from their swelling or from their first contracting and then

---

*One exception to this rule is when you've suddenly removed your favorite vasodilating toxin from your diet—caffeine is the most common. If your blood vessels are dependent on caffeine to dilate them, they get constricted and cranky without their fix, and you can get a severe headache that might last for days and be quite frightening. The best way to get away from caffeine if you are addicted to it is very slowly and incrementally. Even so, you may still experience a dull discomfort in your head for a while.

swelling. The severe pain of migraine headaches probably comes from this kind of fairly rapid change in the caliber of the vessels, from a contracted state to an expanded, swollen one.

Remedies that alleviate the symptoms of headache relax the muscle and return the blood vessels to normal tone, caliber, flexibility, and size. Aspirin (or aspirinlike medications), massage, hot baths, cold compresses, lying down, drinking liquids (without alcohol or caffeine), and sleeping are all things we can do to relieve a headache. Because the release of serotonin in the blood automatically helps contract the blood vessels back to normal size and encourages muscle tissue to return to normal flexibility, anything that promotes a feeling of joy or peacefulness is likely to help a headache.

Preventive measures usually entail eating and drinking more prudently; being more vigilant about toxic surroundings and overscheduling; some sort of regular daily relaxation program, like yoga or meditation; and frequent use of such techniques as biofeedback and imagery.

The exercise I call Imagery to Reinhabit the Body on page 79 turns out to be wonderful imagery for headache, even though it wasn't intended for that purpose. In my workshops, it is often the first exercise I present, and, invariably, when the group shares its responses afterward, several people will tell me, "I had a headache when I got here, and now it's gone."

It makes sense to me that this would be so. Aside from the peaceful, serotonin-producing nature of most imagery, this particular exercise takes the focus of attention from the head, down through the body, all the way to the tips of the toes, using the breath to loosen and dislodge tightness and tension. As a result, tension and blocked energy will move down through the system and away from the head. Simple as it is, it works to release tense head, facial, and neck muscles, and to bring the blood vessels of the head back into balance.

The imagery that I offer you here uses that format but adds more specific headache imagery as well. There is physiological imagery for relaxing muscle and returning blood vessels to their normal shape and size. For good measure, I've included some images of speedy detoxification of overindulged blood and tissue. I also include some simple stretches that assist the release of congested energy in the head, and its rebalance over the rest of the body. If you're in the throes of an intense headache, you probably won't want to move your head. In that case, skip the stretches and just use the imagery. And keep in mind, even the simplest mood-altering imagery, such as remembering your favorite place, is probably going to help your headache.

Imagery for Headache
(approximately 10 minutes)

To begin with, see if you can position yourself as comfortably as you can, shifting your weight so that you're allowing your body to be fully supported. After you take a nice, full breath, try to slowly and gently turn your head to the right, as far as it will go . . . and then breathe out, slowly bringing your head back forward . . . and now, breathing in again, turn your head as far as it will go to the left . . . and as you breathe out, gently turn your head back to looking straight in front of you . . . and now, still very gently, take another breath and lift your chin as far up as it will comfortably go . . . and breathe

*out, returning your chin to its normal position . . .
and taking another breath in, slowly let your chin
drop to your chest . . . and breathe out, returning
your chin to its normal position . . .*

*And now . . . see if you can align your head with
your neck and spine . . . so they are all in a straight
line . . . and your energy can move freely and easily
all the way up and down your spine . . .*

*And gently allowing yourself to turn your atten-
tion inward . . . focusing inside for just this next
while . . . to see how your body feels . . . taking a
gentle, curious inventory . . .*

*Noticing how your body is feeling . . . continuing
to breathe fully and deeply . . . and sensing your
energy level . . . your mood . . . just looking inward
with the neutral, honest eye of a camera . . .*

*Seeing where your body might be tense or tight or
sore . . . and where it feels loose and soft and open
. . . so just letting your awareness move around
inside your body . . . friendly and detached . . .*

*Starting with your head . . . checking to see what
it feels like inside your head . . . noting any tension
or tightness that might be there . . . perhaps just a
congestion of thoughts and worries . . . or an excess
of energy, a busyness in there . . . and on the exhale,
seeing yourself breathing it all out . . . fully and
easily . . . and again . . . noting in a detached way
any tightness in your scalp . . . along the top or at
the base of your skull . . . and feeling it begin to
soften and release . . . as you breathe it out of your
body . . .*

Noting with each breath a gentle softening all through your head . . . a loosening and stretching of the muscle sheath . . . like smoothing soft, friendly sheets over a bed . . . and perhaps even feeling the blood vessels soften, relax, and open . . . returning to their normal width . . . as the tiny muscle bands around them soften and release . . . allowing them to return to their pliable soft texture . . .

Continuing to breathe . . . deeply and easily . . . as you move your awareness down into your neck and shoulders . . . perhaps gently rotating your neck . . . over to your right . . . (pause) . . . and over to your left . . . (pause) . . . breathing into any tight, tense places . . . and feeling the warm energy of the breath . . . warming, loosening, and softening them . . . and gathering up all the tension . . . and breathing it out . . . so that, more and more, you can feel relaxed and easy . . . sensing the subtle stretch and release of muscle and tissue . . .

And taking another deep, full breath . . . as you gently lift your shoulders as high up along your neck as they will comfortably go . . . and as you breathe out . . . rotating them back, softly and slowly . . . letting them settle in place . . . letting them drop into a comfortable, balanced position of their own accord . . . and again . . . breathing in deeply . . . and gently lifting your shoulders as high up on your neck as they will comfortably go . . . and as you breathe out . . . rotating them forward, slowly and easily . . . and again letting them settle softly in place at their most comfortable level . . . so just taking a moment to feel the shift . . . sensing the release of energy all through your neck and across your shoulders . . .

And moving your awareness down into your heart . . . continuing to breathe fully and deeply . . . sensing how it feels around your heart . . . (pause) . . . noticing any heaviness or tightness there . . . as you continue to let the breath warm and loosen and soften any discomfort . . . and sending it out with the exhale . . .

And checking to see how your whole chest feels . . . (pause) . . . moving your awareness around to your back . . . (pause) . . . checking out the entire length of your back . . . (pause) . . . and moving around to the belly . . . looking to see what it feels like in there . . . continuing to breathe deeply and easily . . . noting with friendly but detached interest any tension or tightness in the belly . . .

Breathing into the center of your body . . . wherever you sense that to be . . . (pause) . . . and breathing out . . . (pause) . . . and again . . . deep into the very center of your body . . . (pause) . . . and exhaling fully and easily . . . (pause) . . .

Grateful for your body's ingenious methods of cleansing and clearing itself . . . its filtering of unwanted particles from the blood . . . and sensing the liver and kidneys removing any irritants that might contribute to your discomfort . . . flushing them out . . . efficiently and easily . . . leaving your tissue free and clear . . . light and strong . . .

And continuing to move your awareness down into your bottom . . . seeing how it feels along your whole pelvic floor . . . (pause) . . . noting any tension or discomfort . . . continuing to breathe, deeply and easily . . . maintaining your curious but neutral interest in how your body feels to you . . .

And down into your legs . . . feeling any tightness or rigidity in the legs . . . all the way down to the feet . . . all the way down to the tips of the toes . . .

Just doing this gentle, curious inventory of the inside of your body . . . no praise, no blame . . . just noting where it might feel denser, heavier . . . and where it feels looser and lighter . . . knowing you can use the intelligence of the breath to disperse tension . . . and balance your energy . . . breathing into the core of the tightness . . . letting the breath warm and loosen and soften all around and through it . . . and then breathing the discomfort out, deeply and fully . . .

So just taking this space to reacquaint yourself with this body of yours . . . your steadiest companion . . . your oldest friend . . . and listening to it . . . tuning into it . . . acknowledging it . . .

And letting your awareness sink down into it . . . allowing your spirit to settle all the way down into your body . . . gently and easily letting it float into all your inner spaces . . . all the way down to the tips of your fingers and toes . . . with the soft, easy rolling motion of a thick, rich, misty fog . . .

And just letting yourself feel the fullness of it . . . softly nodding to yourself . . . acknowledging how good it feels to connect back into yourself . . . your energy balanced and even and steady . . .

*And so . . . whenever you are ready . . . taking
another full, deep breath . . . and gently, with soft
eyes . . . coming back into the room whenever you
are ready . . . knowing you are better for this . . .*

And so you are . . .

IMAGERY FOR PAIN

We generally respond to pain in ways that make it
worse. We tighten up and resist it, trying to hold ourselves
away from it. We say no to it with our whole bodies. But
paradoxically, the more we resist it, the worse it gets and
the longer it stays around. Those of us who have used
breathing for pain management during childbirth know
about this paradox. The more we relax and breathe into
each contraction, the less discomfort we have. Of course,
with childbirth we have the advantage of knowing, intel-
lectually at least, that the pain is not signaling that something is wrong, simply that the uterine muscles are
working very hard. And because the contractions usually
have the decency to show up at regular, civilized intervals,
we have the opportunity to recoup our energy, gather our
wits, and renew our readiness to relax around the pain
each time.

A more universal example would be what happens
when we stub a toe. As the pain shoots through us, we
stiffen our bodies, tense our muscles, decry the pain, and
curse the toe. Fear that the toe might be broken tenses us
even more. And the sharp pain has a way of feeding our
fury; most of us will feel intensely and irrationally angry,
either at ourselves for not having seen the offending obsta-
cle or at the miserable lowlife who left it there. This tenses

174

us even more. (Once again our old friend adrenaline is the culprit. If we were needing to flee from the ubiquitous saber-toothed tiger, we'd have the requisite amount of energy to do so. But to be in this kind of extreme alarm state, biochemically armed and dangerous, so to speak, in order to contend with a toy truck on the bedroom floor, clearly shows a certain lack of evolution on our part.)

These responses usually prolong and intensify the pain by increasing muscle tension and internal stress. (If we were contending with the tiger, of course, it wouldn't matter—we'd be in a very focused right-brain state, concentrating too hard to feel pain.)

Psychologically and energetically speaking, we are compartmentalizing the pain: trying to wall it off, hold it away from us, and disown it, in an attempt to get away from it. But we can't get away from it, and this response only intensifies pain. But when we take deep breaths, gently massage the toe, and send kind, calming messages to it—in other words, when we treat our toe the way we would treat one of our own hurt children—the pain does seem to dissolve faster. We dissipate it by joining with it and incorporating it back into us.

Energetically speaking, we want the jarred, separated energy of our wounded toe to rejoin the general flow of the body. It is never in our interest to keep energy withheld from the rest. We are in balance physically and emotionally when every part of us is integrated into the general energetic flow. (See Chapter 2 for a more complete discussion of the idea of energy and how it functions in the body.)

In psychological terms, the same general idea holds true. We can't get past our feelings or our experiences until we can own them, acknowledge them, and accept them. Again the paradox: When we quit fighting with our feelings, we can transcend them. And so with pain.

Imagery that helps with our pain, either chronic or acute, is imagery that interrupts our natural resistance to it and has us softening around it, breathing into it, and, in a sense, befriending it.

Let me state the obvious, though: We need to always investigate why we are in pain, and ascertain that we're not in danger and that we've done what we can do to eliminate its source. Pain is, after all, a signal from the body that something is wrong, a way of warning us to pay attention and respond. If the toe is broken, we might first need to tape it. Then we can practice imagery for the pain.

The pain imagery that follows begins with the mood-altering imagery of the favorite place to help you to relax and get some extra serotonin moving in your bloodstream. (Serotonin is nature's own tranquilizer. It's the neurohormone that helps us become peaceful, and it has painkilling properties as well.) Next, it uses the breath and touch to strengthen the images of softening around the pain, opening to it and then transforming it. Energetic imagery is used so that the narrative can stay general enough to apply to many kinds of pain from many possible sources.

Imagery for Pain
(approximately 11 minutes)

To begin with . . . see if you can position yourself as comfortably as you can, shifting your weight so that you're allowing your body to be well supported. * *You might even want to take a moment to*

*If you are using this imagery for muscular low-back pain, you might want to lie on the floor with your legs over the seat of a chair, thighs at right angles with your body, and your shins parallel to the floor. This gives your lower back maximum support while you "breathe into it" with the imagery.

feel the support beneath you as you adjust your body. Try to arrange it so that your head, neck, and spine are all in alignment.

And taking a deep, full, cleansing breath . . . (pause) . . . exhaling as fully as you comfortably can . . . breathing deep into the belly if you can . . . (pause) . . . and breathing all the way out . . .

And again . . . breathing in . . . and any unwelcome thoughts that come to mind . . . those, too, can be sent out with the breath . . . released with the exhale . . . so that for just a moment, the mind is empty . . . for just a split second, it is free and clear space, and you are blessed with stillness . . .

And any emotions that are rocking around inside . . . those, too, can be noted and acknowledged, and sent out with the breath . . . so that your emotional self can be still and quiet . . . like a lake with no ripples . . .

And now, imagining a place where you feel safe and peaceful and easy . . . a place either real or imaginary . . . a place from your past . . . or somewhere you've always wanted to go . . . it doesn't matter . . . just so it's a place that feels good and safe and peaceful to you . . .

And allowing the place to become real to you . . . looking around you . . . taking the place in with your eyes . . . enjoying the colors . . . the scenery . . . taking in every detail with your eyes . . . over to your right . . . and over to your left . . .

And listening to the sounds of the place . . . whatever they might be . . . the music of moving wind or water . . . birds or crickets . . . just so your ears can become familiar with the sounds of your place . . . that is so safe and peaceful to you . . .

And feeling whatever you're sitting against or lying upon . . . whether it's sand or pine needles or grass . . . you might be in a cozy armchair . . . or maybe sitting on a nice, warm rock in the sun . . .

And feeling the air on your skin . . . either brisk and breezy . . . or soft and still . . . crisp and dry . . . or balmy and wet . . . perhaps you are inside, feeling the warmth of a cozy fire on your face and hands . . . or maybe you are outdoors, and there's just the subtlest caress of a fragrant, gentle breeze . . . so just enjoying the feel of the place on your skin . . .

And smelling its rich fragrance . . . whether it's the soft, full scent of flowers . . . or sharp, salt sea air . . . sweet meadow grass . . . or maybe the pungent smell of peat moss in the woods . . .

So just taking it all in . . . soaking up the richness of it . . . with all of your senses . . . becoming more and more attuned to your special place . . . feeling thankful and happy to be there . . .

Letting your body take in the healing vibrance of the place . . . feeling it penetrate all the way into you . . . soaking into your skin . . . all the way down through muscle and bone . . . all the way to each and every cell . . .

Softly soaking into the places that are tight or tense or sore . . . places where pain is stored . . . and

*feeling the beginnings of a subtle shift deep inside . . .
a softening around the pain . . .*

*And breathing into the pain, you can feel the soft
energy of the breath moving all around and through it
. . . the warmth of the breath massaging and opening
tight, trapped energy . . . and breathing it out . . .
(pause) . . .*

*And again, breathing into the pain . . . with care
and concern for that part of your body . . . soft and
easy . . . letting the gentle energy of the breath caress
and release some of the pain . . . and breathing it
out . . . (pause) . . .*

*And again . . . breathing in . . . and perhaps this
time, if it feels right, and you can, putting your hands
over the place that hurts . . . letting the warmth of
your hands move softly and easily into the pain . . .
encouraging your body to open to it . . . to loosen
around it . . . so it can move more freely . . . and
again, breathing it out . . . (pause) . . .*

*Watching the intelligence of the body . . . as it
softens and opens around the pain . . . giving it more
room to shift and move . . . easing the jagged places
. . . softening constricted muscle . . . dispersing the
heaviness of what aches . . . dissolving the boundaries of the pain . . . and watching its edges disappear
. . . floating out with the breath . . .*

*Feeling the warm, vibrating softness from your
hands . . . gently softening and loosening tension
and tightness . . . slowly and steadily . . . moving
deeper and deeper into the core of the pain . . . gently
releasing as it goes . . . sensing the density of the*

179

pain getting thinner and lighter as its energy expands and floats free . . .

    Continuing to breathe deeply and easily . . . feeling a kind and gentle softness toward yourself . . . a compassion for each and every aching, weary place in your body . . . respect for your own forbearance . . . gratitude for your steady courage . . . taking deep satisfaction in your ability to be present, even under these trying circumstances . . . focused, aware, and fully alive . . .

    Knowing you can always travel with the breath as it moves into the pain on the inhale . . . softening and releasing it . . . (pause) . . . and then feel it carrying the pain out of the body with the exhale . . .

    Always able to touch into the peaceful stillness at your center . . . safe and grounded and connected into yourself . . . steady and centered . . . no longer at odds with any part of you . . . but accepting and allowing it all . . . your body attuned and humming with its own vibrant, healing energy . . .

    And so . . . feeling peaceful and easy . . . you see very clearly that you can call forth this place . . . and the healing power of your breath and your hands . . . whenever you choose to again . . .

    And so . . . wishing your special place goodbye for now . . . you can once again feel yourself sitting in your chair . . . or lying down . . . breathing in and out, very rhythmically and easily . . .

    So gently and with soft eyes . . . coming back into the room whenever you are ready . . . pleased with the powerful resources that are yours to use whenever you wish . . . and knowing you are better for this . . .

And so you are . . .

IMAGERY FOR ALLERGIES

Allergies are hypersensitivities to normal substances that are inhaled, eaten, or brought into contact with your skin. An allergy is a misdirected response of the immune system, which acts as if a harmless substance were a dangerous invading bug or toxin of some sort. Depending on where in your body this takes place, it could show up as asthma, hay fever, hives, celiac disease, or eczema, to name some of the more common ones. Generally, sensitivity runs in families, but it can take many different forms from member to member.

With allergy, the cells of the immune system release irritant chemicals (histamines) that cause such symptoms as inflammation, itching, redness, constriction of airways, excessive production of fluids, fatigue, and headaches.

The best thing to do would be to avoid the allergens that are causing you trouble, but often that isn't possible. Many people get symptomatic relief from medications and other remedies. The imagery that follows should complement those efforts. As with everything else, it's most effective at the first inkling that your allergy is acting up. A full-blown attack is much harder to rout than its beginnings.

Because allergy is an immune system disorder, cellular imagery is appropriate for it. Seeing the white blood cells becoming more selective and less reactive to neutral particles is good cellular imagery. Imagery that helps the physiological symptoms can also help here, whether they appear in the respiratory system, the digestive tract, or the skin. The imagery that follows offers all three possibilities, so you will probably want to choose the symptoms that apply to you.

Psychological imagery also makes sense for allergy. We can extend the notion of hypersensitivity in the immune cells to a kind of hyperreactivity of the whole being, and provide images that encourage a feeling of being more cushioned and less at the mercy of the social environment.

The imagery I offer you here is a variation of the imagery on my asthma tape.* When I first wrote that imagery, I intended to begin it with the device of the favorite place, seeing it as good, standard mood-shifting imagery. But my brother, an asthmatic who is extremely reactive to outdoor allergens, quickly set me straight. He reminded me that just *thinking* about the great outdoors is enough to start him wheezing. So instead, I used a cone of powerful, protective white light that surrounded the listener and kept out irritants from the environment.

Imagery for Allergies
(approximately 8 minutes)

See if you can position yourself as comfortably as you can . . . shifting your weight so that you're allowing your body to be fully supported . . . checking to see that your head, neck, and spine are straight . . . and just taking a moment to feel the support underneath you . . . (pause) . . .

*Health Journeys for People with Asthma, Time Warner AudioBooks, Los Angeles, California, 1993.

And gently allowing your eyes to close . . . and imagining that from somewhere above you . . . a cone of powerful white light is softly and steadily moving down . . . forming a tent of vibrant, tingling energy all around you . . . surrounding and protecting you . . . keeping out anything that might harm or irritate you . . . so you can be safe and comfortable . . . relaxed and easy . . . as you watch the light illuminate everything it touches with exquisite brightness . . . highlit definition . . . vibrating color . . . giving everything it shines on a fresh, new beauty . . .

You can feel the air around you intensifying, glowing, dancing with sparkling energy . . . and with a sense of gentle wonder for such stunning beauty . . . you can feel the tingling energy of the light moving down into your body . . . softly entering your head and neck . . . moving into your shoulders and chest . . .

Feeling the gentle, persistent warmth penetrating into any tightness in the neck and shoulders . . . in the chest . . . slowly, easily loosening, massaging, and opening . . . kneading and softening . . . and continuing down the spine . . . filling your back and torso . . . reaching into every organ . . . into the layers of tissue . . . deeper and deeper . . .

Sending a warm, vibrating softness into any discomfort in the belly . . . gently massaging and opening . . . filling it with powerful, reassuring warmth . . .

And moving down into your legs . . . and filling your feet . . . all the way to the tips of your toes . . .

So just letting yourself feel the vibrant, healing energy of the light . . . working its magic deep inside your body . . . moving with deliberate intelligence to places that feel congested, irritated, or uncomfortable . . . and softly infusing those places with soothing, healing comfort . . .

Feeling it soak into places that are swollen and sore . . . and sensing them begin to shrink back to normal size . . . perhaps opening passageways for breathing . . . gently warming and loosening and widening the airways in the head, neck, and chest . . . softly relaxing tense muscle bands around the tubes . . . and feeling the new space as it opens up . . . making even more room for the gentle flow of sweet, vital air . . . soft and slow and easy . . .

Or perhaps sensing a shift in the swollen feeling in the belly as everything settles back down . . . feeling a warm concentration of the remarkable light soaking directly into any inflamed places in the lining of the stomach or intestines . . . gently shrinking them back to normal size . . . leaching out unneeded fluid and particles . . . smoothing and calming irritated membrane . . . and sensing the linings beginning to subside back to their original shape and form . . . allowing nourishment to again move freely into every part of your body with speed and efficiency . . .

Or perhaps sensing the healing power of the light soothing and calming irritated skin . . . softly returning any reactive patches to their original soft, smooth, pliable texture . . . so that red, scaly, or swollen places are quickly sloughed off . . . and replaced by calm, healthy, new cells . . . growing smooth, soft, healthy skin . . .

And seeing the light . . . like a flare . . . highlighting and magnifying the cells that are accustomed to reacting quickly to irritation . . . and sending them a clear, calming message to settle down . . . and save their energy for the real enemies of the body . . . not these neutral particles that mean no harm . . . and just sensing this reassuring message going directly into the guardian cells of the lungs, the intestines, or the skin . . . wherever it is needed . . . telling them that all is well . . . they can stay ready, but calm and easy . . . able to exercise wisdom and discrimination . . . and able to save their strength for those things that truly harm the body . . .

And understanding that it is not just the cells that are being shown this . . . but that you, too, are settling down . . . developing a balanced sense of calm . . . less reactive to the environment . . . able to save your energy for the real battles . . . more safe and sure, steady, balanced, and strong . . . safely protected in your skin and in the cushion of energy surrounding you . . . attuned to the peaceful stillness at your center . . . stronger and more resilient than you have ever been . . .

And so . . . feeling peaceful and easy . . . relaxed and safe and comfortable . . . infused with light, and feeling all through your body the penetrating warmth and power of this awareness . . . you watch as the light slowly begins to withdraw . . . returning to wherever it came from . . . until it is gone altogether for now . . . knowing it is yours to call forth again . . . whenever you wish . . .

And so . . . feeling yourself sitting in your chair . . . or lying down . . . breathing in and out . . . very rhythmically and easily . . . gently and with soft eyes . . . coming back into the room whenever you are ready . . . knowing you are better for this . . .

And so you are . . .

IMAGERY FOR SLEEPLESSNESS

All of us have experienced insomnia at one time or another. If you are in a persistent pattern that is depleting your resources, you may need a consultation with a health professional. Insomnia can come from depression, anxiety, menopause, pregnancy, overconsumption of caffeine or alcohol, eating a heavy meal late at night, and sometimes from certain kinds of heart and lung disorders. Of course, the older we get, the less sleep we need, and some of us never needed much to begin with. Individual variations are dramatic.

But for most of us, when we can't sleep, it's because our minds are spinning and won't stop. The more we focus on how much we need to be sleeping, the more agitated and wound up we get. Sometimes it makes sense to just get up and get some work done. But for those times when we know we need a good night's sleep, imagery that relaxes the body and refocuses the mind on safety, peacefulness, and calm can be quite effective.* Favorite Place

---

*Actually, many guided imagery tapes, regardless of content, will put people to sleep. Just about every title of the *Health Journeys* series has either been praised or condemned for doing so.

Imagery (page 76) and Imagery to Reinhabit the Body (page 79) will usually do the job, as will the Imagery for Healthy Boundaries (page 153) and the Spiritual Guide Imagery (page 128), because each of these focuses on safety and helps to settle you comfortably down into your body.

The imagery I offer you here combines some of the more powerful elements from each of these exercises, with a focus on encouraging your limbs and whole body to get heavy. As always, I would encourage you to do your own editing of this narrative and insert the things that work best for you. Maybe you won't get to the end of this exercise, because you will have fallen asleep.

Imagery for Sleeplessness
(approximately 9 minutes)

> *To begin with, see if you can position your body as comfortably as you can . . . shifting your weight so that you're allowing your body to be fully supported by the bed underneath you . . . and just letting your body sink down into it . . . letting it get as soft and heavy as it wants to . . .*

> *And taking a nice, full breath . . . inhaling as deeply as you comfortably can . . . breathing all the way into the belly if you can . . . and noticing the turn of the breath as you breathe all the way out . . . fully and easily . . . (pause) . . .*

> *And again, breathing in . . . as fully and easily as you can . . . deep into the abdomen . . . feeling your belly rise with the in breath . . . (pause) . . . and when you breathe out . . . sending tension and*

worry out with the exhale . . . peacefully and easily
. . . (pause) . . .

And again . . . breathing in . . . and sensing the
warm energy of the breath going to any part of your
body that's tense or sore or tight . . . warming and
softening and loosening the tension . . . gathering it
up . . . and breathing it out . . .

So that more and more . . . you can feel safe
and easy . . . relaxed and comfortable . . . sending
the breath to all the tight, tense places . . . to
loosen and warm and soften them . . . and then
use the out breath to release them . . . gently and
easily . . .

And more and more, you can feel safe and comfort-
able . . . relaxed and easy . . . allowing your limbs
to get heavier and heavier . . . letting the weight of
your body sink more and more into the solid support
beneath you . . . as you feel the cleansing action of
the breath . . . with friendly but detached aware-
ness . . .

Aware of the heaviness in your arms . . . the
looseness in your wrists and fingers . . . as they
soften and relax . . . continuing to breathe deeply
and easily . . . letting the remnants of tension there
float free . . .

And aware of the heaviness in your legs . . . the
looseness in your ankles and toes . . . as they soften
and relax . . . continuing to breathe deeply and eas-
ily . . . sending out any remaining discomfort with
the exhale . . .

And noticing the soft, comfortable heaviness in your head . . . a relaxed softness around the forehead and eyebrows . . . feeling a gentle warmth behind your eyes that leaves your lids comfortably heavy . . . and just letting them soften even more . . .

Feeling a softening around your jaw as it loosens and opens with the subtle release of tension around your mouth and ears . . . feeling a warm, comfortable heaviness all through your face . . . as you continue to breathe deeply and easily . . . in and out . . . deep and full . . .

And feeling the warm heaviness move all the way down through your neck and shoulders . . . sensing a soft, comfortable heaviness there . . . as you continue to breathe in and out . . .

Sensing a comfortable heaviness all through your torso . . . as you let go of tension and surrender the weight of your body to the solid support beneath you . . . letting the bed hold you . . . and feeling its support all along your back . . . all along your entire body . . . as you breathe in the warm energy of your breath . . . full and rich and nourishing . . . and feel it turn . . . and breathe out whatever you don't want or need . . .

Aware of a soft, pleasant shift in the belly . . . a softening and letting go of tension as you continue to breathe deeply and easily . . . feeling the warmth of the breath fill your whole abdomen . . . (pause) . . . and then letting it go . . . sensing a pleasant, soft heaviness all through you . . .

And sensing, too, a softness all around you . . . a generous cushion of warmth and protection . . . a gentle sense of safety surrounding you . . . as you continue to breathe deeply and easily into the center of your body . . .

And perhaps even imagining that this cushion of energy is drawing to it all the love and sweetness that anyone has ever felt for you at any time . . . pulling in all the caring and loving kindness that has ever been sent your way . . . every prayer and good wish, permeating and filling the field of energy surrounding you . . . pulling it all in like a powerful magnet . . . calling every good wish and loving thought home . . . to surround and protect you . . .

And perhaps even sensing the presence of all those who have loved you well in the past . . . those who care for you . . . either real or imaginary . . . feeling their protection and support in the warm energy all around you . . . perhaps even seeing a special face . . . hearing a kind, familiar voice . . . feeling a loving touch . . . in your protected, cushioned space . . . continuing to breathe deeply and easily . . . enveloped in softness . . . your body safe and relaxed and easy . . .

Allowing yourself to safely surrender into this feeling of comfort and safety . . . like a dearly loved child, valued and protected, tucked in for the night . . . surrounded by soft quilts and sweet dreams . . . held in the hands of God . . . perfectly, utterly safe . . .

And so you are . . .

IMAGERY FOR FATIGUE
AND A SLUGGISH METABOLISM

This section is for people who feel tired and sluggish too much of the time. The imagery is designed to boost metabolic process and energize the whole system. It can assist with weight maintenance or weight loss, too, though I'm reluctant to emphasize that point. Too many of us already have an irrational and debilitating dislike of our bodies, derived from unrealistic expectations about our weight. Let me be clear that I am in no way suggesting that being thin is inherently desirable. But I do think feeling energized and strong is a worthwhile objective. And imagery that can generate greater acceptance and affection for these weary, faithful bodies of ours is imagery that can do us some good.

I take my cues here from my enlightened twenty-year-old daughter, who was in the kitchen not long ago when I came back from exercising. I was bemoaning the fact that my fifty-year-old body wasn't exactly as lithe as it used to be, and she said with utter sincerity and conviction, "Oh, Mom, you're not *fat*—you're *strong*!" I sometimes marvel at the perspective that this next generation of ours possesses.

As with everything else, if you are tired a lot of the time, you may first want to see your doctor and make sure you have nothing causing it that needs medical attention. You may also want to check out the stressors in your life and make sure you're not overloading yourself with debilitating circumstances and exhausting people. Another possibility is that too much coffee or alcohol for your particular physiology is the culprit. Or you might have a food allergy. A surprising number of people develop an allergy to wheat or dairy products fairly late in life, and this can cause persistent tiredness, a sore, puffy gut, and gas. Sometimes the offending substance is, alas, the food you crave.*

Given those caveats, the imagery that follows is designed to help your body take energy from food with more efficiency, and use it to feel more get-up-and-go. It uses physiological and cellular imagery to encourage your metabolism to perk up, end-state imagery to motivate you to want to move and do more (exercise also energizes you by releasing adrenaline in nice, workable doses), energetic imagery to catalyze the release and flow of blocked energy, and psychological imagery to counter the depressive tendency most of us have to be hypercritical toward ourselves and our own bodies.

Imagery for Fatigue and a Sluggish Metabolism (approximately 11 minutes)

See if you can position yourself as comfortably as you can . . . shifting your weight so that you're allowing your body to be fully supported. Try to arrange it so that your head, neck, and spine are straight . . .

And taking a deep, cleansing breath . . . inhaling as fully as you comfortably can . . . (pause) . . . and exhaling fully . . .

---

*Most physicians aren't geared to think of food allergies as a possibility for adults. But you can check this out yourself by taking yourself off all wheat products (including pasta!) and dairy for a week or two and see how you feel. If nothing is different, you don't have an allergy. But if you find yourself feeling much more energetic and losing weight, you very well could have one. A good, general rule of thumb is that if you are craving the food a lot, you could be allergic to it.

*And again . . . breathing deep into the belly if
you can . . . (pause) . . . and breathing out as completely as possible . . .*

*And once more, sending the warm energy of the
breath to any part of your body that's tense or weary
or sore . . . and releasing the discomfort with the
exhale . . . so you can feel your breath going to all
the uncomfortable, heavy places . . . loosening and
softening them . . . and then gathering up the discomfort and breathing it out . . . so that more and
more you can feel safe and comfortable, relaxed and
easy, watching the cleansing action of the breath . . .
with friendly but detached awareness . . .*

*And any unwelcome thoughts that come to mind,
those, too, can be sent out with the breath . . . released with the exhale . . . so that for just a moment,
it is free and clear space . . . and you are blessed
with stillness . . .*

*And any emotions that are rocking around in
there . . . those, too, are noted and acknowledged,
and sent out with the breath . . . so that your
emotional self can be still and quiet, like a lake
with no ripples . . .*

*And now . . . see if you can imagine from some-
where above you . . . a cone of powerful white light
softly and steadily moving down, forming a tent of
vibrant tingling energy all around you . . . surrounding and protecting you . . . illuminating everything it touches with exquisite brightness . . . highlit
definition . . . vibrating color . . . giving everything
it shines on a fresh, new beauty . . .*

You can feel the air around you intensifying . . . glowing and dancing with sparkling energy . . . and with a sense of gentle wonder for such stunning beauty . . . you feel the tingling energy of the light moving down into your body . . . softly entering your head and neck . . . warming your shoulders . . . allowing them to soften and release . . .

And gently penetrating your chest . . . moving around your heart . . . softly massaging and energizing as it goes . . . steadily kneading and softening and releasing . . .

And continuing down the spine . . . filling your back and torso . . . penetrating into the layers of tissue . . . deeper and deeper . . . slowly and steadily moving into every organ . . . all the way to the bone . . . all the way to each and every cell . . . cleansing and clearing as it goes . . .

Sending a warm, vibrating softness into the belly . . . gently infusing you with the powerful, healing energy of the light . . .

Working its magic deep inside your body . . . moving with deliberate intelligence to all the heavy places where weariness is stored . . . all the way down your legs and into your feet and toes . . .

So just feeling the light move all through your body . . . loosening and energizing the heavy places . . . allowing you to breathe more fully into them . . . and feeling the body begin to charge up with the breath . . . as the movement of nourishing, vital energy spirals wider and wider . . . flowing into every part of your body . . . charging and renewing each and every cell . . .

And sensing the intelligence of the light as it seeks out the glands that determine your body's energy level . . . the tiny but powerful pituitary, the master gland that sits at the base of the brain in the center of your head . . . and the thyroid gland in your neck . . . and feeling the light moving into those glands . . . encouraging them to shift their requirements for energy . . . asking them to command the body to produce more . . . the way we move the lever to reset the carburetor of a car . . . knowing that even a subtle shift will make the engine run faster . . . and use up more gas . . . to avoid stalling . . . understanding that even a small adjustment will make the engine use up more fuel . . . even when it is idling . . .

And so with the body . . . noticing you can sense the well-stocked fat cells of the body gearing up with the promise of increased activity . . . buzzing with energy as they are stimulated by catalysts in the blood that act to break down the fat into very movable particles . . . and just watching those particles pass through the membrane of the cell . . . moving into the muscle and other tissue . . . and so becoming pure energy . . . becoming purposeful motion and life-sustaining warmth . . .

Feeling wonder and gratitude for the remarkable intelligence of the body . . . as you feel the subtle release of energy all through it . . . and the increase of energy flowing through your body . . . freely and

*easily . . . no longer trapped in dense little pockets
. . . but more and more fluid as it moves all through
you . . .*

*And generating more and more the impulse to do
what you love to do . . . freely and easily . . .
without a thought . . . just the mind and body in
free and easy motion . . . fully engaged . . . without
a thought . . . and so just taking a moment to see
yourself involved in doing what you love to do . . .
(pause) . . . and perhaps feeling a new appreciation
and affection for this remarkable body of yours that
always does its best to respond to your wishes . . .
taking you where you want to go . . . your oldest
friend and your steadiest companion . . .*

*And perhaps even seeing it begin to shift its size
and shape . . . as bone becomes stronger . . . muscle
denser . . . feeling your spine grow straighter . . .
feeling fat dissolve as your body more efficiently uses
its resources . . . enlivened cells sparking other
cells . . . a whole contagion of activity that feeds
on itself . . . as more and more you can feel the
increased warmth and energy coming from your
new set point . . .*

*More and more appreciating who you are . . .
softening into who you are becoming . . . as you
also release harsh judgments toward yourself . . .
watching crusty pockets of guilt and self-hatred dissolve and fade away . . . feeling impossible expectations of who you should be and how you should
look melt and shrink away . . . replaced by a new
gentleness toward yourself . . . a permission to be*

who you really are . . . in your own unique and incontestable way . . .

And so . . . feeling light and energized . . . peaceful and easy . . . you watch as the light slowly begins to withdraw and return to wherever it came from . . . until it is gone altogether . . . knowing it is yours to call forth whenever you wish . . . to further the work that you have already done . . .

And understanding that you have done important work . . . that a powerful shift has occurred . . . and will continue to occur . . . you once again feel yourself breathing in and out very rhythmically and easily . . . and so gently and with soft eyes . . . letting yourself come back into the room whenever you are ready . . .

Knowing you are better for this . . .

And so you are . . .

CHAPTER 6

FREQUENTLY ASKED QUESTIONS ABOUT IMAGERY

What is guided imagery?

To review what I've said earlier, guided imagery is a process of deliberately using your imagination to help your mind and body heal, stay well, or perform well. It's a kind of directed, deliberate daydream, a purposeful creation of positive sensory images—sights, sounds, smells, tastes, and feel—in your imagination. For example, you might create images of your immune cells fighting germs or of your pulse rate slowing down; you might recall in exacting sensory detail an absent loved one for extra emotional comfort; or you could "rehearse" a perfect golf swing moments before you actually heft your club. Under the right conditions, your mind and body will believe these images are real, and

will respond accordingly, with varying degrees of efficiency, intensity, and success.

What are some of these "right conditions"?

Being in a relaxed, focused, altered state; using all of
your senses for your imagery, and especially the feeling
sense in the body; continued practice; going to the same
place with the same props each time, at least initially; the
same initial beginning rituals, such as taking two or three
deep breaths; using music for background; the accompanying use of touch, such as putting your hands over your
belly as you breathe; a permissive, unforced atmosphere;
using images that feel right to you, as opposed to imposing
an external idea of "correctness" onto yourself; not trying
too hard, and a willingness to stop for the moment if you
think you are; and, if possible, imaging with a whole group
of people at a workshop or support group, where the
altered-state energy is contagious.

Is guided imagery better than spontaneous reverie states, the kind of unprogrammed daydreaming that we all find ourselves doing during the day?

No, it's not better, just different. We all need to daydream spontaneously. This helps us solve problems, get
in touch with deeper parts of ourselves, and take some
much needed "vacation" time from everyday reality.

Guided imagery, on the other hand, helps us in a
different way, by deliberately helping us impose on our-

selves certain images that we've judged to be good for us.
It's a way of leading ourselves very purposefully to a de-
sired end point.

Ideally, a combination of guided and spontaneous imagery works best. And this is what usually evolves naturally anyway. Repeated listening to a guided imagery
audiotape, or imagining the same sequence over and over
again, frequently results in the imagery seeming to shift
and change of its own accord. Spontaneous imagery that
is more suitable to you and your needs at the time will
replace some of the guided segments.

Is imagery the same as self-hypnosis?

Yes, in a sense it is, although self-hypnosis is really a
broader category that includes verbal suggestion and
thoughts without images. For instance, telling yourself in
the altered state that you will be calm and self-assured
qualifies as self-hypnosis. *Seeing* yourself that way, in
sights, sounds, or feelings, is imagery. Although hypnosis
also uses images, it isn't limited to them.

Some would say that commands and verbal suggestions
under hypnosis work because, at the unconscious level, the
mind is always translating the words into images—that this
is what has to happen for the body to "get it."

How is imagery different from meditation?

Again, meditation is a broader category. You could
say that imagery is a form of meditation. Meditation is any

practice that involves deliberate attentional focus, usually focus on just one thing or a very narrow band of things. This clears the mind, slows it down, and calms, strengthens, and disciplines the meditator. The form of meditation might entail concentration on the breath, or on a single word or phrase; it could be observing every thought and sensation that arises in the mind (often called mindfulness meditation or vipassana); or it could be intense, narrow focus on a simple activity, such as walking, pouring tea, or peeling potatoes.

Imagery involves concentration, too, but strictly on internal sensory images that are deliberately invoked to help with something that's usually fairly specific. And unlike meditation, which usually requires at least twenty minutes at a time, and preferably longer, someone experienced at imagery need only take a few minutes to replay the images they need.

Meditation is usually a practice that is engaged with broader goals in mind. Often they are both spiritual and psychological, designed to help a person adopt a generally flexible, courageous, and gracious attitude toward life, a way of addressing each day with strength and equanimity. Although regular experience with imagery can provide this benefit, too, it is usually utilized to help with a specific worry, ailment, or dilemma.

Many experienced mindfulness meditators become used to having spontaneous imagery pop into their consciousness in the middle of sitting at meditation. This is a natural consequence of leaning into the right side of the brain, in the meditative trance state. But the task of the meditator would be to keep emptying the mind, letting the imagery float away, and watching the next thing that arises. The person using imagery would try to stay with the images and develop them in a directed way.

BELLERUTH NAPARSTEK

How exactly can I use imagery on my own?

One way is to start out using an audiotape, either a professional one or your own recording of one of the scripts in this book. Then put aside a convenient time each day (you'll need at least ten or fifteen minutes for the scripts in this book) to listen in a relaxed, open, attentive state. Most people prefer doing this first thing in the morning or when going to bed at night, or both times each day. Do this for about three or four weeks.

Then, depending more or less on your ability to focus in a relaxed way without falling asleep, you will be pretty solidly connected to the images. At this point you might want to continue with the tape, but without listening so literally.* Instead, you might allow your imagination to take its own flights of fancy, using the narrative as a launching pad to return to if and when needed. The truth is, your imagination might have already begun doing this, with or without your conscious direction.

Another option is to forgo the tape altogether and let your memory invoke the images that are most meaningful to you. You can then let your imagination spontaneously respond with its own variations and inventions. In this way, you can move back and forth from "guided" images to spontaneous ones, in a kind of dialogue between your conscious mind and the deeper parts of yourself. This kind of imagistic "conversation" with yourself may be the most effective, healing use of imagery you can engage in, be-

*Some of you will be like this from the very first time you listen to a "guided" imagery narrative, editing and substituting images as you see fit. But many people have a hard time letting their imaginations go their own way in the face of an already existing structure, or else they just prefer being guided. If this is the case for you, these instructions will make more sense to you.

cause it attunes you to yourself and your body in a very profound way.

Every now and then, it's a good idea to return to the tape, to reestablish a fresh relationship with some of the images and see what you hear after an absence from it. Interestingly enough, at different times, different images will become more compelling to you, and these are the ones to pay attention to.

Another specific way to use imagery on your own is to listen to a particular tape, say for keeping your blood pressure low, until such time as you are solidly familiar with it. You can then "replay" one or two of the more meaningful images through your mind several times a day in very brief (five-second) periods, perhaps whenever you are stopped for a red light or getting ready for a meeting or even brushing your teeth.

You might want to try what the hypnotherapists call an anchoring device, to make this quick replay maximally effective. This involves repeatedly using a deliberately chosen physical gesture whenever you listen to your tape or practice your imagery. After several weeks, you will have developed an instant association to the imagery each time you make the gesture.

For instance, initially, when you are listening to your blood pressure tape, you might choose to put your hands over your belly while you take your deep, abdominal breaths at the start of the exercise. If you do this often enough (usually once or twice a day for two or three weeks), that particular gesture of putting your hands over your belly will become married to your body's response of reducing its blood pressure. After several weeks, you will have a shortcut: When you put your hands on your belly and breathe deeply, your blood pressure will go down, without any intervening effort or imaging on your part. Aren't we humans a wonder?

How often would I need to practice, and for how long?

Usually I advise people to initially "exercise" with imagery for ten to twenty minutes, once or twice a day, for three or four weeks. This really imprints the images and gives you the leeway to get more casual, brief, or ad hoc with them. If you are using a tape, it will usually get stale after a couple of months, and your mind will automatically want to edit or create its own variations on a regularly visited theme. Or you will be ready for a different tape. Either way is fine, depending on your own style and your particular agenda.

How many different kinds of imagery are there?

The possibilities are as limitless as your imagination, but I've conceptualized eight distinct kinds. There's simple imagery to change your mood, what I call *feeling-state imagery*—imagining you're at your favorite vacation spot, for instance. There's *end-state imagery*—imagining yourself the way you want to be but aren't yet, such as diving in perfect form off the board or going back to work feeling strong, energized, and healthy, fully recovered from whatever ails you.

In a more detailed way, you can imagine the cells of your body doing whatever it is they are supposed to do—attacking and demolishing cancer cells, for instance *(cellular imagery)*, or entire organs and body systems functioning optimally, such as your digestive system metabolizing nutrients efficiently and easily *(physiological imagery)*.

You may be more comfortable with symbolic images, like seeing your immune system as a strong and noble army of loyal, committed soldiers, protecting a precious sovereignty—you. This is *metaphoric imagery*.

You can also see your body the way a physicist would, as a system of electromagnetic energy, and imagine its free and healthy flow from stem to stern. I call this *energetic imagery*.

You can engage in imagery that addresses ways to help you process your feelings, or that helps you shift your perception of yourself and others. I call this *psychological imagery*, and this could mean imagining the release of blocked feelings, or seeing yourself with kinder, more forgiving eyes than the ones you've been using. *Spiritual imagery* would be imagery that elicits your sense of communion with the Divine, in whatever form that might take for you—imagining yourself being held in the hands of God or calling up a mystical sense of oneness with all nature.

Is this an ability that some people are born with and others are not?

No. It's an ability that everyone is born with, although it seems to come more naturally to some people than to others. But those who are willing to practice will improve their capacity, regardless of the place they are starting from.

To what kinds of people does this come naturally?

People who have an easy time relaxing or who are generally more "right-brain" will usually find that imagery comes more naturally to them. By "right-brain," I mean people who have a natural affinity for music, emotion, humor, abstraction, intuition, daydreaming, holistic or symbolic thinking, spirituality, and/or creativity.

It also usually comes easier to people who have had to discipline their minds to concentrate very hard on what they are doing at the moment. Professional athletes, dancers, writers, surgeons, craftspeople, artists, and mathematicians would have something of an edge because of their experience with the demand for prolonged attentional focus. Women who have successfully learned Lamaze breathing for childbirth would also have something of a head start.

It comes hardest to people who are uncomfortable with giving up the sense of control that they feel they have when they stay very conscious of their surroundings. Anxious people who characteristically feel a need to stay hyperalert to their environment can have more trouble with imagery, or for that matter, with any technique designed to relax them. So, too, people under a lot of situational stress, people who are survivors of trauma and abuse, and people who were simply born more physically fidgety and mentally distractible than the norm are people more likely to have some initial difficulty with imagery.* But these are also the people who need it the most, and who are very motivated to stay with it until it works for them. And it almost always does. They just might need more time and support to get comfortable with it.

Can children use guided imagery?

Absolutely. Children are naturals at using imagery. They respond to it very easily and very intensely, because they haven't had time to become acculturated away from this natural ability. By adulthood, we Westerners have accumulated so much exposure to a left-brain system of education, and are so saturated with the high value that we place on linear thinking, that some of us have gotten pretty far from imagery. But children are at an advantage.

However, it's important to be sensitive to the age of the child, his or her capacity for sustained attention, as well as the child's level of verbal sophistication. In other words, if the child is young, say under five or six, keep it short and simple. Ten minutes' worth of imagery, spoken in simple, clear language, is more than enough for a young child, whether narrated in person or on an audiotape. Of course, you can take longer if you use an interactive format, asking the child for his or her unique images ("What do you think the fear in your tummy feels like?"), getting responses ("A whole bunch of rabbits jumping around"), and building on them ("Let's ask the rabbits what they

---

*But because there are some surprising exceptions to this rule, don't assume this is so. Because some trauma survivors have used the altered state as an automatic psychological device to protect themselves during the duress they experienced, they can be readily amenable to imagery.

need to calm down and feel safe"). Working like this, the imagery can be devised as you go along, and you may wind up with an imagery story that the child loves hearing repeated, exactly as is, over and over again, or you may have a story that takes different twists and turns each time.

In spite of this oft-cited attention span limitation, many young children show an astonishing capacity for sustained listening. I frequently hear from parents that their seven-, eight-, and nine-year-old children have responded very well to my own rather long-winded imagery tapes, which are filled with fancy vocabulary and elaborate descriptions. In spite of the big words, children seem to get the basic idea anyway, and respond to the voice, the music, and the general feeling tone. They do somehow "get it."

Can imagery really change physiological processes in the body? Is there any proof of this?

Yes, when practiced in the altered state (self-hypnosis), it can. Many studies over the past few years have shown that imagery can heighten immune function; lower blood pressure; speed up healing from cuts, burns, and fractures; and reduce the histamine response to allergies. This names just a few of them.

On the more psychological side of things, other studies show imagery can help alleviate depression, reduce the perception of pain, lower fatigue, and increase relaxation and a sense of well-being.

There are long-term studies in progress now that will tell us more about how well the effects of imagery hold up over time.

How does it work? How could images in the mind actually change the physical body?

The new field of psychoneuroimmunology (PNI) demonstrates that images and thoughts with their accompanying mood states are actually accompanied by alterations in the biochemistry of the body. Images appear to activate the nervous system, sending neurohormones (chemical messengers) through the bloodstream to specific cells, where they trigger healing activity.

In a sense, the new discoveries require a profound shift in our thinking about ourselves. Because what all of this really means is that *the mind is not limited to the brain; the mind is part and parcel of the whole body.*

On a less biochemical note, you could say that imagery works because the body doesn't altogether distinguish between images and real events, especially if the images are highly sensory and evocative. And in a good, strong altered state (a trance or reverie state) the images can be quite potent and real to the body. So when we access this altered state, and in it create healing sensory images, the body to some degree believes they are real events, happening both inside and outside of it.

Is imagery a reasonable alternative for standard medical treatment?

No. Maybe someday, when we know more about how to consistently and fully harness the power of our minds, but not yet. Right now, imagery is best used as *adjunctive treatment.* Of course, for some health problems, there's not a whole lot else available. But mostly, it's a good form of complementary medicine, not an alternative form of therapy. In fact, it works very well with standard Western medical treatment. Imagery is usually a subtle and gentle intervention that makes its impact incrementally over time. If someone were to be rolled into an emergency room, bleeding profusely from a gunshot wound, imagery clearly would not be the treatment of choice. The wonderful techniques and machines of Western medicine would do the job, although imagery would be helpful in calming the patient. It would help him stabilize his blood pressure, cope with pain, and connect with his motivation to stay alive. Imagery is a beautiful complement to heroic, emergency room measures, empowering the patient to be part of his own treatment.

Because of its gentle, incremental nature, imagery probably works best as preventive medicine. It is most powerful over time, helping to keep the body's systems tuned and running. When illness does strike, the person has a highly developed skill base from which to fight back.

Does it work better for some conditions than for others?

The truth is that there haven't been enough studies to answer this question properly. We're just beginning to understand some of what imagery can do through careful, long-term research. For instance, we know for certain that it works well to help alleviate emotional states like anxiety and depression. We know that it can help boost immune system functioning, and so it probably will have positive long-term effects on cancer and HIV. And studies are currently under way to see what it can do for various autoimmune diseases (illnesses that involve overactive or misdirected immune cells, attacking the body's own tissue), such as M.S., rheumatoid arthritis, and asthma. My own clinical evidence for autoimmune disease is extremely encouraging. I probably get more heartfelt thank-you letters from tape users with autoimmune disease than any other health category. But soon enough we'll all know much more, because so many fine studies are currently under way.

Do I need to be well versed in physiology to use imagery properly?

For some kinds, yes. For others, no. Some kinds of imagery require an accurate knowledge of physical body process—imagery that involves the cells and imagery that involves the organs of the body, what I call cellular and physiological imagery. When using this kind of concrete, physical detail, it's best to have done your homework, because you don't want to mistakenly suggest something to your body that runs counter to its own best interests. Although you don't have to know exactly what your organs look like, you do need to know how they work and what they are supposed to do. The same is true for your cells. So for this kind of imagery, you should talk to your doctor or nurse specialist, or get to the library and read up on your condition. And if you are taking medication, you need to understand what that is doing for you, too.

However, there are other kinds of imagery, equally effective, that don't require this kind of conscientious research. End-state imagery, for instance, only asks that you know what you want to achieve and that you be realistic;

metaphoric imagery has you imagining things in their symbolic form; and feeling-state imagery has you shifting your mood in a very general way.

Can I use guided imagery to help me cope with anxiety over an anticipated situation, like taking a test, auditioning for a part, or preparing for an interview?

Yes, imagery is very helpful for this. There are three ways to use it. One is to simply imagine, with as much concrete detail as you can gather in advance, a successful experience. This entails imagining the room, the other people there, and all the sights, sounds, smells, and even tastes of the situation, including the position and feel of your own body there. You do this over and over, replaying a successful outcome.

Another way to do this is to imagine a supportive presence with you when you are there, both in advance of and during the anticipated situation. This could be your idea of a guardian angel; it could be Grampa, who is long gone but who always adored you; or it might be an inspiring teacher who believed in what you could do. Again, these images should be summoned up in all their sensory detail. Most important, you want to *feel* their presence with you.

And third, you can prepare yourself by remembering a time when you felt very triumphant and strong, a time when you did yourself proud. Again, this should be recalled in all its concrete, sensory detail, reliving it in your mind to the point where you are again flooded with the "high" feelings that you had then. When these feelings are at maximum intensity, use any unobtrusive anchoring device: squeeze your fist; place your palms together; put your hands over your belly as you breathe deeply. Choose whatever suits you. Do this repeatedly. Then, when the situation is at hand, very briefly use your anchoring device and let it transport you to those feelings of confidence and triumph.

Whenever I relax, I fall asleep. How can I prevent this while I'm using my imagery?

Try sitting up with your back away from the chair and your eyelids half-open. If that doesn't work, try it walking at a relaxed, meditative pace. If you stay with it, at some point your body will be able to make the transition to being both relaxed and awake at the same time.

Is it true that if you fall asleep listening to a tape, your mind is still hearing it at some level anyway?

I don't know of any definitive studies that prove this to be the case with regard to normal sleeping, but there have been studies showing that surgery patients under anesthesia hear what is said during the operation. If that is the case during a drugged sleep, I would certainly think it to be so for normal sleep. And surely if you listen to a tape *repeatedly*, your brain will eventually take in much of its content.

Most experts say, and I agree, that the ideal mode of listening is with *relaxed but focused attention*. But listening asleep is better than not listening at all.

Often during an imagery exercise, my attention wanders, and sometimes I don't even know where I've "gone." Is this normal?

Yes, normal and commonplace, too. "Paying attention" in the altered state, using the right side of the brain for guided imagery, has a very different quality to it than the sharply focused, left-brain attention we give to, say, studying a report. In the trance state, we float in and out of awareness, in the gentle, receptive mode that allows imagery to happen.

Once we've noticed that we've been "elsewhere," all we need do is gently guide ourselves back to the imagery. There's no such thing as "blowing it" on the right side of the brain. We can only scold ourselves on the left.

Often during an imagery exercise, I'll start to cry. Should this worry me?

No. It's typical and normal for the eyes to tear up. In fact, many people also get runny noses and a desire to cough as well. Although the experience may be quite different for different people, it usually means one of two things: Either you are moved by the experience of relaxing, settling down, and getting back in touch with yourself, and your tears are a reflection of the warm, full feelings that this generates, or else you've been so busy racing around, fulfilling your day-to-day responsibilities, that you haven't given yourself the space to release your everyday feelings. Settling into your imagery allows you to rinse out the top layer. Either way, it's very good for you.

Sometimes I feel dizzy after working with my imagery. Am I doing something wrong?

If you are a generally healthy person, no. This just means you aren't yet used to moving back and forth from a regular waking state to a deep altered state and then back again. After some practice, this transition will get much smoother.

In the meantime, it might help if, during your imagery, you intermittently turn your attention to the feel of your feet on the floor or your back against the chair. This concrete reminder of the boundaries of your body and the physical support of your surroundings will help hold you steady, and modulate the effects of the "motion sickness" generated by your traveling imagination.

Can guided imagery ever be bad for me?

Probably *anything that's effective can be misused*, so yes, imagery could possibly be bad for you. If you mistakenly work with a physiological imagery exercise that runs counter to what's right for your body, you can work against yourself. The damage would be subtle and incremental (just as positive gains from imagery are) and would take repeated experiences to make its presence felt, but eventually it would. So you always want physiologically based imagery to be accurate and informed.

The same holds true for psychological imagery. Your assumptions need to be correct. If your operating assumption is that it is desirable for you to cut yourself off from your uncomfortable feelings, and you devised imagery in the service of that outcome, it would not be good for you, because it's a bad idea in the first place.

Luckily, we have within us an ingenious fail-safe capacity that sometimes goes to work for us. The mind will often produce, of its own volition, spontaneous imagery that corrects the inaccuracy and sets the balance right. It will sometimes do this even when you have no conscious awareness of what is happening.

Sometimes people will experience spontaneous imagery that frightens them, and they will think that because it's unpleasant, it's bad for them. Actually, this is the unconscious mind offering up some valuable information. It needs to be processed by writing about it in a journal or talking about it with a friend or a professional psychotherapist. Perhaps more imaging is needed to get beyond the initial reaction. But in most cases, it's better to lean into this kind of experience rather than retreat from it.

Imagery can be bad for you if you use it in place of effective medical treatment, because you'll be denying yourself the benefits of some powerful therapies.

It can be bad for you if you use it while driving or operating machinery, because it usurps your attention and makes those activities dangerous.

And finally, imagery is bad for you when you use it to avoid taking responsibility for your life. The imagination is a fabulous gift and an amazing tool. It enriches our lives and extends our capacity for all manner of things. But it should never seduce us away from taking care of ourselves in normal, waking reality. It's no substitute for grounded, sensible living.

RESOURCES

GUIDED IMAGERY AUDIOTAPES

Health Journeys, by Belleruth Naparstek, L.I.S.W., Time Warner AudioBooks, 9229 Sunset Boulevard, Los Angeles, CA 90069. General Wellness, Depression, Grief, Relationship, Stress, Pain, Headache, Back Pain, Cancer, HIV, Multiple Sclerosis, Rheumatoid Arthritis & Lupus, High Blood Pressure & Heart Disease, Asthma, Diabetes, Stroke, Surgery and Chemotherapy.

The Source Cassette Learning System, by Emmett Miller, M.D., 945 Evelyn St., Menlo Park, CA 94025. Change the Channel on Pain, Down with High Blood Pressure, Easing into Sleep, Headache Relief, Healing Journey, Health and Wellness, Smoke No More.

Mind Works (for children ages 4–12), by Roxanne Daleo, Ph.D., P.O. Box 2493, Cambridge, MA 02238. The Star Within, The Healing Heart, Good Night.

Meditations for Everyday Living, by Bernie Siegel, M.D., ECaP, 1302 Chapel Street, New Haven, CT 06511 (203-865-8392). Meditations for Enhancing Your Immune System, Meditations for Everyday Living, Meditations for Finding the Key to Good Health, Meditations for Morning and Evening, Meditations for Overcoming Life's Stresses and Strains, Meditations for Peace of Mind.

The Bodymind Audio Tape Program, by Jeanne Achterberg, Ph.D., New Era Media / The Arc Group, P.O. Box 410685-BT, San Francisco, CA (914-141-0685). Cancer, HIV, Diabetes, Hypertension, Rheumatoid Arthritis, Insomnia, Migraine, General Relaxation, Pain, Immune System Enhancement, Slimming.

Changeworks Cassettes, by Thomas Condon, Ph.D., P.O. Box 5909, Bend, OR 97708 (800-937-7771). Rapid Pain Control, Deep Sleep and Sweet Dreams, Getting Past Smoking, Sensible Weight Loss, Quick Stress Busters, Natural Self-Confidence, Creative Personal Power, Creative Problem Solving. Free catalogue.

GUIDED IMAGERY WORKSHOPS AND SEMINARS

Academy for Guided Imagery, P.O. Box 2070, Mill Valley, CA 94942; Martin Rossman, M.D., and David Bresler, Ph.D., Codirectors.

The Bonny Foundation, 2020 Simmons St., Salina, KS 67401; Helen Lindquist Bonny, Ph.D., CMT, Director.

OTHER RESOURCES

Two national experts on the practical, clinical uses of guided imagery with patient and employee populations are:

Eileen Durham, R.N., Coordinator, Relaxation and Imagery Program, Lucile Salter Packard Children's Hospital at Stanford, 725 Welch Road, Palo Alto, CA 94304 (415-495-8900).

Julie T. Lusk, M.Ed., Director, Health Management Center, Lewis-Gale Clinic, Salem, VA 24153 (703-772-3750).

BOOKS ABOUT GUIDED IMAGERY

Becker, Robert, and Gary Seldon. 1985. *The Body Electric*. New York: William Morrow.

Brown, Barbara. 1980. *Supermind*. New York: Bantam.

Durham, Eileen, and Cindy Cooper. 1989. *Therapeutic Relaxation and Imagery Development Manual*. Cupertino, CA: Health Horizons.

Epstein, Gerald. 1989. *Healing Visualizations*. New York: Bantam.

Fanning, Patrick. 1988. *Visualization for Change*. Oakland, CA: New Harbinger.

Gendlin, Eugene. 1979. *Focusing*. New York: Bantam.

Levine, Stephen. 1987. *Healing into Life and Death*. New York: Doubleday.

Lusk, Julie, ed. 1992. *30 Scripts for Relaxation, Imagery and Inner Healing*. 2 vols. Duluth: Whole Person Associates.

Moen, Larry, ed. 1992. *Guided Imagery*. 2 vols. Naples: United States Publishing.

Nilsson, Lennart. 1985. *The Body Victorious*. New York: Delacorte.

Ornstein, Robert, and David Sobel. 1987. *The Healing Mind*. New York: Simon & Schuster.

Porter, Garrett, and Patricia Norris. 1988. *I Choose Life*. Walpole, NH: Stillpoint Press.

Rossman, Martin. 1987. *Healing Yourself*. New York: Pocket Books.

Samuels, Michael. 1990. *Healing with the Mind's Eye*. New York: Summit Books.

ABOUT *HEALTH JOURNEYS* AUDIOTAPES

Since 1990 Belleruth Naparstek has been producing guided imagery audiotapes to help people with specific health conditions and medical procedures. These tapes are based on the principles and clinical information discussed in this book. The series is called *Health Journeys*, and is available on Time Warner AudioBooks. So far, current titles include the following:

For Specific Health Conditions

For People with Asthma
For People with Cancer
For People with Diabetes
For People with High Blood Pressure/Heart Disease
For People with HIV Infection
For People with Multiple Sclerosis
For People with Rheumatoid Arthritis/Lupus
For People Recovering from Stroke
For People with Headaches (two tape set)

For Medical Procedures

For People Undergoing Chemotherapy
For People Undergoing Surgery (two tape set)

For Psychological Issues

For People with Depression
For People Experiencing Grief
For People Working on Their Relationship (two tape set)

For General Health

For Anyone Concerned with General Wellness
For People Coping with Pain
For People Experiencing Stress (two tape set)

For inquiries about Belleruth Naparstek's speaking schedule, or for questions, feedback, or requests for new tapes, please call or write Image Paths, Inc., at 2635 Payne Avenue, Cleveland, Ohio 44114, or call (800) 800-8661.

INDEX

INDEX